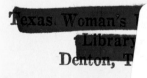

ch/w

THE MODERN LANGUAGE ASSOCIATION OF AMERICA

GENERAL SERIES

XI

WILLIAM CONGREVE, THE MAN

Approved for publication in the General Series of the Modern Language Association of America

ERNEST BERNBAUM
E. PRESTON DARGAN
HOWARD MUMFORD JONES
WILLIAM KURRELMEYER
KEMP MALONE
EDWIN B. WILLIAMS

Committee on
Research Activities

Published under a grant awarded by the American Council of Learned Societies from a fund provided by the Carnegie Corporation of New York

Will: Congreve.

THE YOUNG DRAMATIST

WILLIAM CONGREVE
THE MAN

A Biography from New Sources

BY

JOHN C. HODGES

NEW YORK: MODERN LANGUAGE ASSOCIATION OF AMERICA

1941

Reprinted with the permission of the original publisher

KRAUS REPRINT CORPORATION

New York

1966

Printed in U.S.A.

To
LILIAN NELSON HODGES

CONTENTS

ILLUSTRATIONS

FOREWORD

I

WHEN Edmund Gosse, in 1888, wrote the first comprehensive biography of William Congreve, he was convinced that "unless fresh material should most unexpectedly turn up, the opportunity for preparing a full and picturesque life of this poet has wholly passed away." On revising the life in 1924, Gosse found that the intervening thirty-five years had added practically nothing to the known facts about Congreve, and regretted the continued lack of fresh sources out of which the author of *The Way of the World* might be interpreted as a human being. Other biographers have since appeared, but even the latest of them regrets that the individuality of Congreve is obscured by "an almost impenetrable veil."

It is not surprising, then, that the leading article of *The Times Literary Supplement* for September 25, 1937, speaks of William Congreve, the "man of superb genius," as also "the man of mystery." To his contemporaries, however, Congreve was no man of mystery. Dryden found him a personable young law student who could ably assist either in the translating of Juvenal or in the making of a contract with Tonson. Swift passed many a pleasant evening with this "very agreeable companion." Lady Mary Wortley Montagu declared Congreve the wittiest of all her acquaintances. Pope believed him "most honest hearted," and Steele praised his congeniality in no uncertain terms. "No one," he wrote, "after a joyfull Evening, can reflect upon an Expression of Mr. Congreve's that dwells upon him with Pain."

Few writers have had more generous and more discriminating critical appreciation. John Dryden, Dr. Johnson, William Hazlitt, George Meredith, and Bonamy Dobrée—these and many others have done justice to the creator of Millamant and Sailor Ben. But they have told us almost nothing of the boy whose inheritance, environment, and training fitted him as a very young man to delight London's popular audiences and to win over its most severe critic. Nor has anything substantial come to light concerning the personal circumstances of the older man who, after a few active years, tried in vain to slip away into a retirement secure from gossip and acclaim.

To the mass of critical appreciation already available this biography adds nothing directly. But it does attempt to make possible a more discerning and more sympathetic reading of Congreve by bringing from fresh sources new information about the boy and the man.

Congreve's background and early development help to explain the phenomenal success of his early work. Hardly less important is a just understanding of his later motives, for certain things he did—often reported but consistently misinterpreted during the last two hundred years—have left the impression that Congreve was affected, snobbish, and untrustworthy. Merely in justice to his work, it is high time to attempt a fuller view of the antecedents, characteristics, and motives of Congreve the man.

II

New material about Congreve has not been easy to find. There is no central storehouse of information, no large accumulation of letters, no helpful journal to which the biographer may turn. But tucked away here and there in the original manuscripts in England and Ireland—most of them never before examined by students of Congreve—there are many telling bits of information. Other documents by or about Congreve have been brought to America and are now in public libraries or in the hands of private collectors scattered from New England to California. No one of these fresh sources, by itself, goes far toward giving a full-length picture; but the new details, fitted together and interpreted, do much to fill out the portrait and to clarify features that have annoyed and puzzled students for two centuries.

Even the identity of Congreve's mother has been uncertain. None of the numerous biographical sketches of the dramatist appearing during the eighteenth century so much as mentions her. After 1800 she is variously referred to as Anne Fitzherbert, Mary Nicolls, Anne Browning, or Mary Browning. Gosse was never able to decide between Anne Fitzherbert and someone bearing "the maiden name of Browning." The most recent biographer, D. Crane Taylor, gives only passing mention to Congreve's mother as "Mary Browning whose family was somewhat obscure."

Congreve himself provided the key to the problem in the account of his life which he furnished to *The Poetical Register*. Giles Jacob, editor of the *Register*, applied to Congreve for assistance and received the following reply:

Surrey-street, July 7, 1719

Sir,

I much approve the Usefulness of your Work; any Morning, about Eleven, I shall be very ready to give you the Account of my own poor Trifles and Self, or any thing else that has fallen within the compass of my Knowledge, relating to any of my Poetical Friends.

I am, Sir,
Your Humble Servant,
William Congreve

In the resulting sketch of Congreve's life, apparently supplied by
the dramatist himself, occurs this sentence: "He was born at a place
call'd *Bardsa*, not far from *Leeds* in *Yorkshire;* being a part of the
Estate of Sir *John Lewis*, his Great Uncle by his Mother's Side."
A very little investigation at that time would have shown Congreve's
connections, through his mother, with the prominent Lewis family of
Yorkshire. But the eighteenth century, led by Dr. Johnson, dis-
credited Congreve's claim to birth in Yorkshire and therefore paid
little heed to what Congreve said about his family connections there.
Fortunately it is still possible, by means of wills and other documents,
to identify Congreve's mother, to trace her ancestry, and—more important—to show something of what the dramatist inherited from
her.

Although more has been known of the family of Congreve's father,
the Congreves of Staffordshire, the dramatist's relations to them have
never been adequately traced through the family papers preserved in
Stafford and through the detailed family genealogy kept in the handwriting of each generation since the sixteenth century. Without this
genealogy it has hitherto proved difficult to distinguish between the
dramatist and his four contemporary kinsmen also named William
Congreve. The signed documents of one William Congreve have
been widely collected and prized as those of the celebrated dramatist.
Today at least six American libraries have among their manuscripts
certain papers of this cousin erroneously ascribed to the dramatist.

From manuscripts still preserved at Kilkenny and Dublin it is
possible to trace Congreve's boyhood in Ireland. The records of the
Irish army show the wanderings of Congreve's father the lieutenant,
and his little family, from the seaport of Youghal in the southeast to
distant Carrickfergus, near Belfast; and then south again to the
brilliant and cultivated life of Kilkenny, and finally back to Youghal.
Municipal records of the Irish towns, and notes and pen sketches of
contemporary travelers in Ireland, picture the environment in which
young Congreve lived. New light on his school days at Kilkenny is
shed by the manuscript notes of the school's patron and by the records of Congreve's schoolmaster.

More important still are the various manuscript records preserved
at Trinity College, Dublin. Thanks to these, Congreve's college years
are no longer a blank. The voluminous minutebook of Provost and
Fellows—with its record of punishments, awards, and miscellaneous
academic affairs—leaves no doubt as to the atmosphere in which
Congreve spent his three years at college.

But the most significant document is the college *Buttery Book*,

Junior, Novr. 1685 to Octr. 1687. Here Congreve's name is set down forty-one times. Here, in a mass of information about purchases from cellar and kitchen, about fines for missing chapel, disputations, or the early morning lecture in science—here for the first time we have something really personal about the young man who was soon to win the plaudits of London with *The Old Bachelor.* As we see the contacts of the young college student with the flourishing theatre near-by in Smock Alley, we wonder a little less at the phenomenal success of his first comedy in Drury Lane.

A few years ago Joseph Wood Krutch rightly called attention to our inadequate knowledge of Congreve as a government official, noting that "it is not certain how abundantly he shared in the governmental favors then showered upon literary people." For this reason, I have searched the documents at the Public Record Office—the final authority in such matters—to determine the nature and extent of Congreve's public service.

It is impossible in a short preface to enumerate all the fresh materials drawn upon. Yet mention should be made of the ledgers of Messrs. Hoare & Company, who kept "running cashes" in Congreve's day, and of the Bank of England, and of Tom Twining's Coffee House (all doing business as usual today)—for all these have made their contributions. To these must be added miscellaneous documents of the South Sea Company, numerous wills, and other legal papers. Such documents help to give an intimate picture of Congreve at his simple lodgings in the Strand, or at the luxurious homes of his friends and fellows among the Kit-Cats.

Additional letters by Congreve have long been exceedingly difficult to find. Consequently, the eight new letters printed in this life, from widely scattered sources, will be welcome. Four new portraits of Congreve, reproduced from the original paintings, tell their own story. These show the dramatist at the age of twelve, twenty-three, thirty-four, and thirty-eight. The dates of these portraits make them more significant than the two well known paintings by Kneller, both of which are from a later period, long after Congreve had completed the work for which he is remembered. The portrait at the age of twelve, the original of which is now hanging at Chartley Hall, Staffordshire, furnishes in a note by the artist the exact date of Congreve's birth—a matter that has been in dispute for over two hundred years.

The new material here utilized has made possible the correction of many errors of long standing. For the most part, these corrections are made without comment, but the authority in each case is given in the notes.

III

Anyone who reads the many contemporary statements about Congreve's qualities as a man, and then, in chronological order, the scores of biographical sketches that appeared during the next two centuries, cannot help recognizing that, as time went on, Congreve the man—as distinguished from the dramatist—became progressively more distasteful to his biographers. By the end of the nineteenth century the Victorians had pictured him as so lacking in force and character that to Gosse he was "no very fascinating or absorbing human being." Dryden, Swift, and Pope would not have recognized in this new Congreve the man they had known so well.

The phenomenal decline of Congreve's reputation as a man began in the eighteenth century. Throughout that century he was censured as an inglorious example of an eminent man whose pride had led him meanly to deny the country of his birth. Dr. Johnson avoided the specific accusation that Congreve had falsified the place of his birth but damned him effectively with the remark that "it was said by himself that he owed his nativity to England, and by everybody else that he was born in Ireland." Then, to drive his point home, Johnson took a whole paragraph to lament the fact that men of eminence are often "very deficient in candour," and lightly tell "falsehoods of convenience from which no evil immediately ensues except the general degradation of human testimony."

Finally, at the end of the century, the record of baptism proved that Congreve was born in Yorkshire, as he had said, and that "everybody else" was wrong. But a century of repeated accusation had made its impression. Posterity had come to think of Congreve as proud and insincere. The very registry that proved him honest as regards the place of his birth was now hailed as positive proof that he had lied about the time. For the record showed baptism in February, 1670, whereas 1672 had long been the accepted year. Nobody took the trouble to discover that the year 1672 as that of Congreve's birth was first specifically mentioned in print the year after his death, and that, on the one and only occasion when he is on record as mentioning it, Congreve gave his correct age.

Another strong factor against Congreve's reputation has been the ill-considered but influential snap-judgment of Voltaire, who once visited Congreve and thought him exceedingly vain because he spoke of his works as "trifles" and wished to be visited "upon no other Foot than that of a Gentleman, who led a Life of Plainness and Simplicity." This story has seldom been overlooked in even the shortest sketches of Congreve's life, while few indeed have remembered the calm estimate of Swift, who knew Congreve intimately from his school days. Vanity was never charged against Congreve by Dryden, Pope, or by anyone else intimately acquainted with him. Except for the fact that posterity had already come to think of Congreve as vain and insincere, it would have seen the injustice of accepting the estimate of a passing foreigner so utterly inconsistent with the expressed opinions of those who knew Congreve best.

IV

Probably the chief cause of the decline and fall of Congreve's personal reputation has been his hitherto unexplained, and apparently strangely capricious, conduct toward the two women with whom he was most intimately associated—Anne Bracegirdle and Henrietta, Duchess of Marlborough.

All London had heard of Congreve's infatuation with charming Anne Bracegirdle, the darling and the reputed Diana of the Restoration stage. And London also knew that afterwards, for some obscure reason, Congreve transferred his attentions to the young Duchess of Marlborough—was with her at the watering places, at her Lodge in Windsor Park, and at her city home in St. James's Square. Immediately after his death the town gossiped about how "very particular" the Duchess had been on Mr. Congreve's account, and how she had shown "so great an affection for his dead body that she quitted her house and sat by his corpse till he was interred."

These were choice bits for the gossips. Soon the unprincipled Curll had in his press a book with a scandalously alluring title—*Memoirs of the Life, Writings, and Amours of William Congreve, Esq.* Mrs. Bracegirdle was concerned enough to demand a sight of the manuscript. Her request was refused and, according to the writer of the Preface, "she then wanted to know by what Authority Mr. *Congreve's* Life was written, and what Pieces were contain'd in it that were genuine? Upon being civilly told, there would be found several Essays, Letters and Characters of that Gentleman's writing, she with a most affected, contradictory, Dramatick-drawl, cry'd out, *Not one single Sheet of Paper I dare to swear.*"

The Duchess was equally concerned and wished, in addition, to stop the printing of Congreve's will, in which she was the chief beneficiary. But Curll declared that he valued "neither the Messages nor Threats, either of Peer or Peasant," and pretended to dismiss them as mere *"Drawcansir-*Bullyings." Notwithstanding this assumed boldness, Curll did not dare carry to the extreme his affront of the great lady. He did not print the gossip about her. Indeed, he did not justify the alluring title of his book. If he knew the true circumstances—and he probably did not—he failed to show how Anne Bracegirdle and the Duchess had fitted into Congreve's life, why Congreve had made a will in which he left so little to the one and so much to the other, who could not possibly have needed it.

And so, for two centuries, this will involving Congreve's relations with the two women who meant most to him has been thought strange and inexplicable, or else a "ridiculous" instance of extreme pride and worldliness. If not a part of the Congreve "mystery," it may be said to be the one more or less substantial skeleton which has remained hidden in his closet.

Fortunately documents are still preserved which permit us to bring the skeleton into the open, to explain the actions that have been hitherto so puzzling. Oddly enough, the very will which has helped to shroud Congreve in ungrateful mystery through the years, now studied for the first time in the light of such documents as Duchess Henrietta's will, becomes the medium from which Congreve emerges, an understandable man acting from very human motives.

To most of those who have made available to me manuscript collections in England, Ireland, and America, or who have liberally assisted in other ways, I must remain silently grateful except as I can remember them in the notes. Some more fundamental obligations are recorded here. I must express thanks to Miss Annabel Hodges for the map of Congreve's London; to Professor John Robert Moore for assistance in the placing of landmarks; to Mr. Stewart Robertson for helpful advice; to Malcolm Elwin, Esquire, for kindly allowing me to examine his important manuscript work on Congreve; and to Mr. Carl Sandburg, who has read some chapters of this biography while it was in preparation and has given helpful suggestions. More particularly I am indebted to the untiring assistance, the wide scholarship, and the discriminating taste of my friend Professor Alwin Thaler.

Sir Geoffrey Congreve, Bart., has generously placed at my disposal the Congreve family genealogy in the sixteenth, seventeenth, and eighteenth century manuscripts, has given permission for the reproduction of Congreve portraits in his collection, and has granted free use of the materials he has gathered for a history of his family. To the American Council of Learned Societies I express deep appreciation for assistance which has made possible the publication of this biography. Finally I gratefully acknowledge the assistance of my son Nelson, who has been my companion in tracing Congreve through Ireland and England and has touched vitally many parts of the work.

CHAPTER I

PROLOGUE IN YORKSHIRE

I

THREE quarters of a century before William Congreve was born at Bardsey in Yorkshire, his great-great-grandfather Timothy Bright was rector at the neighboring village of Barwick-in-Elmet. Queen Elizabeth was just completing her long reign, and it was she who had preferred him to this Yorkshire post. Dr. Bright was already past middle age. As a lad of eleven, in 1561, he had entered Trinity College, Cambridge, and seven years later had taken the degree of bachelor of arts. Thereafter he earned two medical degrees and a license to practice his profession. In the midst of his duties at St. Bartholomew's Hospital, he found time to write medical treatises, one of which he dedicated to Sir Philip Sidney.

Dr. Timothy Bright was a philosopher as well as a physician. His true bent appeared in his *Treatise of Melancholie, Containing the causes therof, & reasons of the strange effects it worketh in our minds and bodies: with the physicke cure, and spirituall consolation for such as haue thereto adioyned an afflicted conscience* (London, 1568). Whether or not this was, as it has been supposed, the inspiration for Burton's *Anatomy of Melancholy*, at least it revealed the author's interest in philosophical reflection. Timothy Bright was a man to welcome the privacy of a village rectory. He abandoned medicine, took holy orders, and was granted a living in Yorkshire. This appointment came after he had won the favor of his practical queen by dedicating to her his *Characterie. An Arte of shorte, swifte, and secrete writing by character*—in other words, the invention of modern shorthand.

At Barwick-in-Elmet, just east of the city of Leeds, Timothy Bright spent the last twenty years of his life. He turned from Plato, in Greek and Latin versions, to books in Hebrew and Syriac, and studied Italian music. He had an Irish harp which he "most usuallye played upon."[1] Sometimes he piped on his theorbo, a flute-like instrument that is mentioned in his great-great-grandson's novel *Incognita*. It was an old instrument which seems to have died out

[1] From the will of Timothy Bright, dated 9 August 1615, as published in *Yorkshire Arch. Jour.*, XVII (1902–03), 52–54. For the facts of Bright's life, and for his significance as inventor of modern shorthand, see *DNB*.

along with this antique breed of gentlemen who could assimilate all
the branches of science in one mind. Dr. Bright's fame as a splendid,
if incalculable, asset to the district survived him down the years. As
late as the eighteenth century it was told how at one time, in a
pleasant intellectual haze, he had turned and asked his steward to
buy some oxen grazing in the open field, forgetting that these same
oxen already belonged to him.[2]

When Timothy Bright, B.A., M.B., Lic. Med., M.D., rector of
Methley and Barwick-in-Elmet, died in 1615, he left to future generations of his family his best though least tangible asset, the fine tradition of a useful and richly cultivated life. His worldly possessions he
had neatly disposed of in his will. To his brother, a clergyman, he gave
his Irish harp, one of his two theorbos, some books on music, a
Hebrew Bible, a Syriac Testament, and the works of Plato. To his
younger son Titus, a physician, he left all of his "books of Physick
and Philosophie." He had previously given his estate, so his will indicated, to his oldest son Timothy, a barrister living twenty miles
farther south in Yorkshire near Doncaster.

This older son had studied law at Gray's Inn and had been admitted to the bar in 1608. In the same year he married Edith Lewis, of
the old and prominent county families of Lewis and Reresby. Nine
years later the barrister and his wife died within a few weeks of each
other, leaving four young children in the care of their uncle Thomas
Lewis at the family manor at Marr near Doncaster.[3]

One of these four orphans was Mary Bright. By 1635 she was the
wife of Walter Browning, a young clergyman in residence at Don-
nington Chapel, Yorkshire, a few miles south of Doncaster. Walter
had been a poor boy, studying at King's College, Cambridge; and he
had not grown wealthy during the five years after he received his
master's degree. Before he died in 1636 he made a will in which he
urgently tried to make his little estate provide for the needs of his
young daughter Mary. It was then nearly a century before Defoe
was to startle his own generation by proposing seriously to educate
women; and yet this Yorkshire clergyman left the whole of his meagre
fortune for the "education" and care of "Marie my daughter."[4] Just

---

[2] *Publications of the Thoresby Soc.*, XXI (1912), 185.

[3] For the lawyer Timothy Bright see the "Register of Admissions to Gray's Inn,"
Collectanea Genealogica, ed. Joseph Foster (London, 1881), p. 101; Yorks. Arch. Soc.,
Record Series, XXXIV (1904),118. For the pedigree of the Bright family and the will
of Edith Lewis Bright, see Joseph Hunter, *South Yorkshire, the History and Topog-
raphy of the Deanery of Doncaster, in the Diocese and County of York* (London, 1828),
I, 365.

[4] See the will, dated 7 June 1636 and probated by Mary Browning, widow, on 18

how adequately the will of the earnest young clergyman was executed we do not know. If his wishes were carried out, and if his daughter Mary Browning, who was to be the mother of William Congreve, did receive an education better than average, it was only fitting for one whose father, whose grandfather, and whose great-grandfather had devoted themselves to the learned professions.

A few years after Walter Browning died, his widow married Dr. George Roe of Doncaster.[5] And so it was that Mary Browning grew to womanhood in the peaceful home of a physician in South Yorkshire. It was the period of the Civil War, but it is not likely that the stress and turmoil of those years invaded the quiet home of the physician in Doncaster.

II

Far different was it just sixty miles south at the home of the Congreves in Staffordshire. William Congreve, the lad who was to be the father of the dramatist, was only five years old when the Civil War opened in 1642.[6] His father, Richard Congreve, was the prosperous squire of Stretton Hall and a staunch Royalist—fair game for the Roundheads of Oliver Cromwell. In 1643 they raided the Stretton estate. They drove off Richard's horses and his cattle; they robbed him of his money, and even of clothing. Again the following year they returned to rob and pilfer, and yet again and again during the period of civil strife. Indeed, the losses which Richard Congreve sustained at this time because of his "steady attachment to the Royal cause in the great rebellion" were to be keenly felt in the years to come.[7]

One of Richard's younger brothers was slain in battle, and two others fought valiantly for King Charles throughout the war. The

December 1638, Somerset House, P. C. C., Lee 181. See also the entries for Walter Browning in *Alumni Cantabrigienses*, compiled by John Venn and J. A. Venn (Cambridge, 1922 ff.); and Hunter, *South Yorkshire*, I, 138.

[5] Mary Bright Browning was still a "widow" when she probated her first husband's will at the end of 1638. Her first child by her second husband, Dr. Roe, was baptized on 3 April 1640. See Hunter, *South Yorkshire*, I, 365.

[6] Information about the Congreves of Staffordshire is derived chiefly from the manuscript record of the family now in possession of Sir Geoffrey Congreve, Bart., of Chartley Hall, Stafford, through whose kindness I have been permitted to examine the document. The manuscript is called the *Erdswick Book* because it was begun by Sampson Erdswick, the historian, about 1593. It gives a mass of information about the Congreve family not available elsewhere and is, of course, the chief authority for the family genealogy. It is difficult to understand why this important manuscript has been hitherto overlooked by the biographers of Congreve the poet.

[7] See the *Congreve Family Papers*, William Salt Library, Stafford, and Br Mus. Add. MS. 16,569, ff. 66, 67. The first raid was made in 1643 and others followed in 1644, 1645, 1646, and 1647.

Congreves never wavered in their loyalty, even when all seemed lost with the establishment of the Commonwealth. After the disastrous battle of Worcester, in 1651, Richard Congreve aided the twenty-one-year-old Charles II to escape from Cromwell's men. The young King would almost certainly have fallen into Cromwell's hands but for the loyality of thirteen Staffordshire squires who hid him well near Stretton Hall.[8]

From a very early period the paternal ancestors of the dramatist had resided at the hamlet of Congreve in Staffordshire. Early in the fourteenth century Simon de Congreve married his son to Catherine Schampion and through her acquired the more important estate of Stretton. Nine generations later, in 1633, Richard Congreve married Anne Fitzherbert of Norbury in Derbyshire. In the old *Erdswick Book*, the manuscript in which the Congreve family has kept its history generation by generation, Richard wrote down the record of his twelve children. Elizabeth and Martha were born at Norbury in 1634 and 1635; John at Stretton in 1636. Then follows the entry for William, who according to a note in a later hand, "married Mary, dau. of Walter Browning of the County of Norfolk," and became the father of the dramatist. The original entry in Richard's handwriting is as follows:

> William
> h. 3.20 P.M. was born at Stretton 17 september 1637.
> William, Earle of Newcastle
> William Perpoint of Tonge Castle Esq
> The Lady Dorothy Fitzherbert of Norbury were Gossipps.

This Earl of Newcastle who assisted at the christening was William Cavendish (1592–1676), the patron of Ben Jonson, and later of Dryden. After the Restoration he was created the first Duke of Newcastle. William Perpoint, or Pierrepont (1607?–1678), was the grandfather of the first Duke of Kingston, whose daughter was the famous Lady Mary Wortley Montagu.

Born a year after his brother John, William Congreve the elder was thus narrowly shut out of the Stretton estate of six hundred pounds a year. He could not be lord of the manor; and he did not choose, like his younger brother Thomas, to matriculate at Cam-

---

[8] King Charles II never consummated his first generous intention of establishing a new order of Knights of the Royal Oak to honor the thirteen loyal squires who made possible his escape. He did, however, present Richard Congreve with a painting of a court beauty by Lely, which is still preserved at Chartley Hall. For a list of the thirteen persons intended for the knighthood see *Collections for a History of Staffordshire*, William Salt Arch. Soc. (1920–22), p. 129.

RICHARD CONGREVE, 1609–1689
Congreve's Grandfather at Stretton Hall

bridge. Instead, he did what was more common among the younger sons of the Congreves: he entered the army. The depleted condition in which the Congreve estate was left by the Civil War made it all the more important that William look about him for a means of livelihood.

III

The period of the war and the Commonwealth was much kinder to the Lewises of Yorkshire, the family in which Mary Browning's mother had been reared. As Mary Browning grew up in Doncaster, she must have seen much of her Lewis cousins only five miles away at Marr. Edward Lewis, the older son, stayed on at Marr to take his place as head of the family while the younger John Lewis went away to seek his fortune in India and Persia. The very years that were heaping misfortunes on the Congreves were bringing great wealth to John Lewis.[9] He even became, it was said, a familiar of the Persian Shah. Back in London, he married the daughter of Sir Thomas Foote, Lord Mayor of London. He was knighted by Charles II at the Hague, and after the Restoration he was created a baronet. Pepys mentioned him as one of the "great merchants" he met in the spring of 1662.

Sir John Lewis kept a town house in Lincoln's Inn Fields and also built up a large estate in his native Yorkshire. His chief seat was at Ledstone Park, about fifteen miles north of Marr. His two daughters —his only children—were married, one to Theophilus Hastings, seventh Earl of Huntingdon, and the other to Robert Leke, third Earl of Scarsdale.

Whether William Congreve, Esquire, came a-wooing Mary Browning at her mother's home in Doncaster, at the old Lewis manor nearby, at Sir John Lewis' estate of Ledstone Park, or at his London home in Lincoln's Inn Fields, we do not know. Perhaps he met her first in London and continued to court her in Yorkshire. At any rate, William Congreve and his wife Mary were living on a part of Sir John Lewis' Yorkshire estate, at Bardsey, when their son William was born.

Bardsey lies ten miles northwest of Ledstone Park. The hamlet, situated in pleasantly rolling country, clusters about a grassy, oblong knoll whose green shoulders betray the remnants of an old Roman camp. At one side of this knoll, where the ground begins to slope more gently, rest the brown stones of Bardsey Grange, flanked by numerous outhouses and an old mill. The Grange was the manor house of the

[9] G. E. C., *Complete Baronetage* (Exeter, 1900 ff.), III (1903), 126. See also Hunter, *South Yorkshire*, I, 361; Hist. MSS. Com., *Hastings MSS.*, I (1928), 402; Pepys, *Diary*, 22 March 1661/2.

village, with a history that can be traced far back to the year 1204, when King John confirmed it to the monks of Kirkstall Abbey. John Lewis had purchased the Grange in 1654 and had opened it to Francis Thorpe, one of Cromwell's barons of the exchequer, who had lived there until his death in 1665.[10] Then Sir John had made it available to his cousin Mary and her husband William Congreve.

During those early years of the Restoration, English society was in a state of change. No longer did the groundlings flock to the theatre as in the days of Marlowe and Shakespeare. No longer were the masses a chief concern of the playwrights. The appetites of the repatriated courtiers who returned with King Charles II in 1660 had been whetted by the sophisticated plays of the French theatre. Light, witty comedies of Molière were the vogue in Paris. Soon London audiences demanded the same sort of fare, and the new dramatists, quick to sense the taste of the town, were eager to supply what their sophisticated audiences wanted. Precisely at this time of transition in English society the Congreves, then living at Bardsey, were daily expecting the birth of a child. He proved to be William Congreve the dramatist, destined to act a leading part in that society, to observe its foibles and its shallowness, and to etch it indelibly in our most polished comedies.

William Congreve was born on Sunday, the twenty-fourth day of January, 1670.[11] After two and a half weeks in the old manor house at the foot of Castle Hill, he was taken around to the opposite side of the hill, to the quaint, square-towered Church of All Saints. There he was baptized by the Reverend John Fentiman, who had been chosen as rector nine years before by Sir John Lewis.[12]

[10] For the history of Bardsey and the Grange see John Burton, *Monasticon Eboracense* (York, 1758), p. 290; Edmond Malone, *Dryden* (London, 1800), I, 225, note; R. V. Taylor, *Ecclesiae Leodienses* (London, 1875), pp. 139–146; T. D. Whitaker, *Loidis and Elmete* (Leeds, 1816), pp. 160–163. The parish register of the Bardsey Church of All Saints records the burial of Thomas Thorpe on 7 June 1665.

[11] The exact date of Congreve's birth has been hitherto unknown. The date here given is that painted by the artist Clarea at the lower left corner of the portrait of Congreve at the age of twelve. The eighteenth-century opinion that Congreve was not born until 1671 or 1672 was corrected long ago by Malone's discovery of the record of baptism. Recent biographers, however, are not satisfied that the baptism indicates the approximate time of the birth. They hold that the birth occurred in 1669, the year before the baptism. The error on which this opinion is based I had already pointed out in *Modern Philology*, XXXIII (1935), 83–85, before discovering on the Clarea portrait what seems to be the exact date of Congreve's birth.

[12] Whitaker, *Loidis and Elmete*, pp. 160–163. The parish register records the baptism as follows: "William the sonne of Mr William Congreve of Bardsey Grange was baptized Febru: 10th, 1669 [1670.]"

The Congreves did not remain long at Bardsey Grange. By 1672 they were in London, where they buried their daughter Elizabeth at St. Paul's in Covent Garden on the twenty-second of September.[13] Nothing is definitely known of their children other than William and Elizabeth, but the dramatist's mention of himself as "the only surviving son"[14] implies that there were others who died in childhood.

In the autumn of the next year—on October 17, 1673—the father secured a passport to the Low Countries.[15] He was executing a commission to buy coach horses for his Royal Highness, the Duke of York, in Flanders, Holland, and Germany. Whether his wife and young son accompanied him we do not know. Early the following year he was again in England, making plans that were to take him and his little family to Ireland for the next fifteen years.

The Irish army which William Congreve the elder was now about to join had already seen much of the Congreves. At least four of his uncles had served in Ireland, and one of them, Edward Congreve, had fallen in battle there. Another, Francis Congreve, had been one of the guards of the Duke of Ormond, Lord Lieutenant of Ireland, and had attained the rank of colonel before his death in 1662. A third, Captain John Congreve, according to the inscription on his tomb, served Charles I and Charles II "from the first Rebellion in Ireld, in all their warrs to the time of his death" on August 7, 1670.[16] The fourth of these uncles, Captain Christopher Congreve (1622–1706), was still on active duty in Ireland. He had gone over about 1663 to command one of the independent companies of infantry. Later he was taken into a regimented company and became successively major and lieutenant colonel before he was retired on a pension in 1687. During a part of 1673 Captain Christopher was back in England, and it may be that uncle and nephew then put their heads together over vacancies in the Irish regiments. Whatever the source of

---

[13] See the parish register of St. Paul's, as published by the Harleian Soc., XXXVI (1908), p. 60.

[14] Giles Jacob, *The Poetical Register* (London, 1719), p. 41. The information in the first part of Jacob's account of Congreve was apparently furnished by the dramatist himself.

[15] Public Record Office, State Papers Domestic, Entry Book 40, p. 122.

[16] See "Gregory King's Note Book" for 11 August 1680, *Collections*, William Salt Arch. Soc. (1919), p. 220. Extensive records of members of the Congreve family in the Irish army, especially for Colonel Christopher Congreve, have been preserved in the Ormonde Manuscripts. Some of these are made available by the report of the Hist. MSS. Commission, but many are to be found only in the original MSS., which are preserved partly at Kilkenny Castle, Ireland (*Army List, Chiefly Irish, 1598–1714*), and partly among the Carte MSS. in the Bodleian.

the nephew's commission, it was granted on March 19, 1674, three days after Captain John Boteler had certified that William Congreve was "very fit to serve as lieutenant of a foot company,"[17] and the lieutenant set out with his captain to garrison the thriving Irish seaport of Youghal.

The lieutenant's son was then but four years old. For the next fifteen years young William Congreve was to live and learn in a society which, according to the usual view, was far removed from the culture and the graces of the court.

[17] P. R. O., S. P. Dom., Car. II. 360, No. 234. For the commission see S. P. Dom., Entry Book 35 A, f. 87. Lieutenant Congreve reached Youghal in time to be listed for the quarter ending 22 March 1674/75. See the manuscript *Army List, Chiefly Irish, 1598–1714*, preserved in the muniment room of Kilkenny Castle.

CHAPTER II

AT YOUGHAL AND KILKENNY

I

IN 1674 Youghal was one of the more important Irish seaports, the first to which the English merchantmen came as they sailed westward out of the Bristol Channel. The town hugged one side of the busy harbor at the mouth of the Blackwater River and sent its little streets up the hillside on which rested the collegiate Church of St. Mary's and the myrtle-covered gables under which Sir Walter Raleigh had resided as mayor of Youghal.[1] Around the whole in a large semicircle ran the medieval wall. It swept up from the harbor to the top of the hill, extended along the crest back of the church, and came down again to meet the water.

Within this old town lay the Desmond earls buried under their effigies. They had passed on, these flashing Geraldines. Monuments of their piety and their zeal for learning rose at either boundary of the town in the ruins of the Franciscan and the Dominican monasteries, and clear, fresh rays of sunlight now played through the slender windows of the crumbling transepts. Almost untouched by time's decay remained the Desmond "College of Our Lady of Youghal," its buildings standing up finely by the old Church of St. Mary's; but its singing men and its wardens were gone.

For a century before the Congreves came, the Desmonds had been only a memory. Sir Walter Raleigh had ended that dynasty, and Sir

---

[1] The effort made in this chapter to reconstruct the busy little seaport of Youghal as Congreve would have known it is based chiefly upon (1) the extended description and pen sketches made by Thomas Dingley, an English lawyer, during his visit to Youghal about 1681 (*Observations on a Voyage Through The Kingdom of Ireland. Being a collection of Several Monuments Inscriptions draughts of Towns Castles &c.* National Library of Ireland MS. 392, pp. 215–236; partly reproduced in *Jour. of Kilkenny and South-East of Ireland Arch. Soc.*, 1862–63, pp. 320 ff.); (2) a seventeenth-century map of Youghal reproduced in *Pacata Hibernia*, III; (3) an early drawing of "The Towne and Port of Youghall," Trinity College, Dublin, M. S. 1209, No. 67; (4) a very interesting oil painting of Youghal, evidently of the sixteenth or seventeenth century, now owned by Mr. William Murphy, 56 North Main Street, Youghal; (5) the researches of Samuel Hayman as recorded in *The Annals of Youghal* (Youghal, 1848), and his later revisions and additions; and (6) careful observations made by the author during a ten-day stay in Youghal.

9

Walter in turn had given way to the Boyles. Richard Boyle had landed in Ireland with twenty-seven pounds in his pocket, and a new era had begun: an Elizabethan culture had replaced the chivalry of the Desmonds. Richard Boyle bought the Tudor mansion in which Sir Walter had lived and the many thousands of Irish acres which Queen Elizabeth had granted to her favorite. The new owner managed his affairs so astutely that Richard Boyle, barrister, became Sir Richard, then Baron Boyle of Youghal, and finally Earl of Cork. He built ironworks and he cut down the forests. Four thousand laborers worked his plantations. Thirteen strong castles went up to protect his empire. And when he died at Youghal in 1643, some muttered "Robber Boyle," some "the great Earl of Cork." They buried him in St. Mary's under his effigy in gilt and black armor, with his fifteen children in red sandstone praying at his feet.

The first Earl had lived at Youghal, in the old Desmond College on the hillside by the Church. He had so developed it that "its faire Roomes, with well wrought Chimney pieces," and its "extreame pleasant"[2] garden were the admiration of visitors to Youghal throughout the period of the Congreves. Richard Boyle, the second Earl of Cork, was then the master. He lived sometimes at Youghal, sometimes at near-by Lismore Castle, and at other times on the Clifford estates in Yorkshire, which were now his through marriage. He had also acquired the English title of Earl of Burlington.

The first Earl of Cork had been too busy building his empire to think much of the humanities. His kinswoman, however, married Edmund Spenser; and among his children and grandchildren appeared writers and patrons of literature. One son was Robert Boyle, the philosopher. Another was Roger Boyle, first Earl of Orrery, who together with Dryden rhymed tragedy into popularity in the early Restoration years. This old fighter, politician, and dramatist was living near Youghal when the Congreves arrived. Five years later he lay by the side of his father in St. Mary's Church.[3]

Between the Congreves and the Boyles sprang up such friendly relations that the younger William years later dedicated his first play to Charles Boyle, eldest son of the second Earl of Cork, and spoke feelingly of "the particular Ties, by which I am bound to your Lordship and Family." Possibly the two families had first become acquainted in Yorkshire, and in such a way that William Congreve the elder had some business reasons for securing an army appointment at

---

[2] Dingley's *Observations*, National Library of Ireland MS. 392, p. 219.

[3] The Register of St. Mary's Church, Youghal, reads as follows: "1679. October ye 18 Roger boyle Earll of orrery was buried."

Youghal. It is known that not only "his Command in the Army carried him into *Ireland*," but also "his Affairs." If he did have some means of subsistence other than his lieutenantcy, it was well, since he could not be sure of his monthly salary of five pounds and twelve shillings.[4] Irish monies had a way of leaking from the treasury. Viscount Ranelagh, favored rascal of Charles II, was fleecing the Irish to fill his own pockets and the privy purse of the King. Lieutenant Congreve suffered among others: the second year after he arrived in Youghal the King owed him nine months back pay.[5]

The Congreves remained at Youghal for five years, and it is probable that young William had his first schooling there. "The Free School here," wrote a contemporary visitor to Youghal, "is the Guift of the said Rt Honble Sr Richard Boyle Knt, Lord Boyle, Baron of this town, &c., Earle of Cork. It hath a Master and Usher, who have salaries of thirty and ten pounds p an. for ever, and a good house, Rent free."[6] This house, originally provided by the first Earl of Cork about 1634, was used as a grammar school for nearly three centuries. The school house of grey stones and mortar lodged the master on the first floor. From the rear, where the playing field lay, stone steps led up to the study room on the second floor. There the master and the usher assembled the sons of the officers, the younger generation of the Boyles, and other youngsters whose parents wished to have them prepared for the university. The school was but a stone's throw from the bustling harbor. Looking from the windows of the schoolroom on the second floor, the boys could see a dozen sails of boats from England, Germany, Holland, and the Indies.[7]

Toward the close of 1678, when young William was nearing his ninth birthday, his father was transferred to Carrickfergus, far

[4] The salary of a lieutenant in the Irish army is shown by the military list for the year beginning 25 March 1676, *Plantation Papers*, Trinity College, Dublin, MS. F. 3. 15. Another military list (T. C. D. MS. E. 1. 1) shows that the salary remained the same as late as 1688.

[5] Richard Bagwell, *Ireland under the Stuarts and during the Interregnum* (London, 1916), III, 119–121.

[6] Dingley, *Observations*. The original building in which the first Earl of Cork established the free school about 1634 stood until 1924. My description of the building is based upon the memories of Mr. John E. Farrell, an old resident who attended the school, and upon the statements of others who knew it well.

[7] Ships from these four countries are specifically mentioned by Dingley, who referred to Youghal as a "famous Port." An abstract of Irish customs for the year beginning 25 March 1681 (T. C. D. MS. F. 3. 15) gave Youghal eighth place among the sixteen ports listed. In the same list Carrickfergus was even more important, taking fourth place. Unquestionably Youghal and Carrickfergus were busy ports during Congreve's period in Ireland.

away on the northeastern coast of Ireland. William remained there
for three full years, thus rounding out the most impressionable years
of his boyhood. Carrickfergus was even a busier port than Youghal,
yielding more than ten thousand pounds yearly to the King's customs.
The little town was filled with English sailors, rough and jovial
fellows. Memories of eight years spent at Youghal and Carrickfergus
may well account for some of the salty flavor one finds in Sailor Ben,
the "absolute Sea-Wit," of *Love for Love*.

At Carrickfergus William's father was still a lieutenant at sixty-
seven pounds and four shillings yearly. It was here that for the first
time in Ireland he joined his Uncle Christopher Congreve, who was
captain of the company with the rank of major. Near the end of 1681,
uncle and nephew came south to join the regiment of the Duke of
Ormond at Kilkenny, and young William entered the great preparatory school endowed by the Duke.[8]

II

Young Congreve encountered a vastly different life at Kilkenny. In
the seaports the hard and difficult side of life was visible. The cargoes
of the merchantmen demanded sturdy backs and strong hands, and
the sharp, reddened faces on the docks were hard-bitten by the rough
winds of the world. At Kilkenny, on the other hand, the air was calm,
almost serene. Even a twelve-year-old boy might have been impressed
by the elegance and importance of the place after the freedom of
Youghal and Carrickfergus. At Kilkenny the Irish twang gave way to
a more distinct English accent; the roughened faces assumed English
contours and faded from red to white. Here, too, was breeding far
above what William had been used to. He himself, the lieutenant's
son, could not have been an ungracious boy; but here one might be
put to shame by the courtesy of even the ragged flour carriers. They
drove their squeaking wagons under the castle walls and, brushing
too near a passer-by, would apologize with the gentlest of manners.[9]

___

[8] Lieutenant William Congreve's various places of residence in Ireland can be determined by means of the Ormond army records preserved at Kilkenny Castle (a
MS entitled *Army List, Chiefly Irish, 1598–1714*) and at the Bodleian Library (*Revenue
and Army of Ireland*, Carte MS. 54). It should be noted that the Hist. MSS. Com.
reports on the Ormond manuscripts at Kilkenny Castle omit many of the references
to Lieutenant Congreve.

[9] An eighteenth-century traveler writes of Kilkenny: "Walking one Day by the
side of the River, near some Corn-Mills, I was met by a Flour-car: the Driver who
was seated on the Thill, was a mean looking, ragged Youth. Just as I had passed him,
he accidentally dropped his Rod out of his Hand; when another Youth, of nearly the
same Complexion with himself, coming along the Road, readily stepped aside, took

It was not by chance that Kilkenny had come to be the most polite and well-bred of all the Irish towns. For centuries it had been a place of consequence in Irish history, the seat of more than one Parliament. It was the chief residence of the Earls and Dukes of Ormond, hereditary Butlers of Ireland. These gentlemen had been repeatedly Lord Lieutenants of the kingdom and had kept at Kilkenny Castle a viceregal state that gave dignity to the whole of the little city. When Congreve came with his father to Kilkenny, the Ormonds were at their gorgeous best. At that time they were headed by James, the first Duke, who was esteemed "the richest subject of any monarch in Europe."

It is not hard to imagine the effect of Kilkenny upon the boy. He saw it at a time when, like a small but clear pool, it reflected the concentrated pomp of Whitehall and St. James's. It lacked neither fine gentlemen nor elegant ladies. Gentlemen flocked from Ireland and England to spend months at the Castle and wait upon his Grace. Nor did Kilkenny lack entertainment. Bull baiting, popular there since Elizabeth's day, had its "Mayor of the Bull-ring" as late as 1687. The royal game of tennis, so much enjoyed by Charles II, was a favorite sport of its citizens throughout the seventeenth century. There was bowling, both at the Castle and in the town. And on special occasions the players came down from the Smock Alley Theatre, Dublin, "with all their appurtenances . . . to entertain ye company" at the Duke's Castle.[10]

We get a picture of the ladies in a portrait that Lely did of the wife of the young heir. She is a woman quite of the Restoration style which Congreve was later to do so well, cleverly bold of eye, radiant in crimson silk, attended by a little black boy. She has in her look much of the audacity which is continually an element in Congreve's heroines, something a little stronger than mere impudence, something perhaps of the boldness of rococo. She lived by fountains of black marble, in halls blazing with gilded leather, under ceilings shimmering with angels.

Her dwelling, Ormond Castle, is described by Thomas Dingley,

---

up the Rod and, very politely, presented it to Owner. This occasioned many Compliments. Monsieur himself could not have made a better Leg than the Presenter. Each waved his Hat—bowed—recovered—turned—then parted and covered.—Instances of this Sort may be observed hourly in the Streets of Kilkenny; which show that they are beforehand with their neighbors, the English, in the fine Art of Politeness." See the *Jour. of the Kilkenny and South-East of Ireland Arch. Soc.* (1862–63), p. 107.

[10] See the manuscript notes on Ireland by John Dunton, Bodleian MS. Rawl. D. 71. f. 25; also, John G. A. Prim, "Olden Popular Pastimes of Kilkenny," *Kilkenny Arch. Jour.*, II (1852–53), 319–335.

the London lawyer who was at Kilkenny a year before Congreve: "Ye Castle of Kilkenny . . . famous for spacious Roomes, Galleries, Halls, adorn'd with paintings of great Masters, Bowling Green, Gardens, Walks."[11] A few years later John Dunton, London bookseller and editor of the *Athenian Mercury*, visited the Castle and declared the grounds "finer than the *Privy-Garden* in *Whitehall*."[12] He was enraptured by the "*Noble Gallery*, which, for length, variety of gilded Chairs, and the *curious Pictures* that adorn it, has no equal in the Three Kingdoms, and perhaps not in Europe." Among the furnishings were no less than twenty-five suites of tapestries, including a "suite of Antwerp hangings, containing Seaven peeces of the Story of Dietius, thirteene foote deepe," and others portraying the stores of "Achilles," "Octavius Cesar," "Aswerus & Hester," "Cyrus," and "Don Quixott."[13]

The Duke had a larger income than several European monarchs. He lavished a two-thousand-pound dinner upon the English King. And when for a time the Duke lapsed from favor at Whitehall, Buckingham remarked that it was hard to say whether the Duke of Ormond was in disgrace with the King or the King with the Duke.

III

Ormond power, as we have said, was at its zenith when Congreve came to live within the shadow of the Duke's court. The newcomer was nearly twelve, just the right age for entering the "great School or College of Kilkenny." Once his father was settled as an officer in the Duke's regiment, it was inevitable that William should attend the Duke's school.[14] Not only was it one of the best in the British

---

[11] *Observations*, pp. 202, 203.   [12] *The Dublin Scuffle* (London, 1669), p. 373.

[13] See the several inventories for the furniture of the Duke of Ormond in Ireland for the years 1675, 1684, 1689, as discussed by the Rev. James Graves, "Ancient Tapestry of Kilkenny Castle," *Trans. of the Kilkenny Arch. Soc.*, II (1852), 3–9.

[14] "A List of the Commissioned Officers . . . in Ireland," in the Bodleian Carte MS. 54, shows that Major Christopher Congreve and Lieutenant William Congreve were quartered at Carrickfergus for the three months ending 25 September 1681; and the Army List at Kilkenny Castle mentions these same officers as belonging to one of the four companies quartered at Kilkenny for the three months ending 20 Aprli 1682. Since their quarters are not mentioned for the last three months of 1681, it is evident that the transfer from Carrickfergus to Kilkenny was being made at that period. The Register of Kilkenny College, begun in 1684, naturally has no reference to the date of Congreve's admission. A list of those leaving the school, begun in the same year, mentions Congreve's withdrawal in April, 1686. The Register shows that the boys who matriculated during Congreve's period were from nine to fifteen years of age, the average being twelve. It is interesting to note that Congreve specified twelve years as the age at which the hero of his novel *Incognita* entered school at Siena.

Isles, but it was thrown open free to William under its charter, which
read, "Children of all such as are attending in the service of the
duke of Ormond, shall at all times be admitted to the privileges and
benefits of said school gratis."[15] The Kilkenny scholars might even
hope for preferment through the Duke. While Congreve was enrolled
in the school, Lodowick Jackson, of Youghal, wrote about his son
whom he had "kept at Kilkenny School" and whom he thought
"fitted by his small growth, and other education, to wait on his Grace
or his Lady Duchess as page, or to attend Lord Ossory [the Duke's
son] in his travels."[16]

In a painting of that day the grounds of the school stand out distinctly, hugging the western bank of the little River Nore and over-
shadowed across those quiet waters by the Ormond castle walls.[17]
Many a morning Congreve, having begun the school day at six, must
have watched the sun rise over those battlements. The rest of the
town, a maze of ashy grey walls, houses, and old churches with
perpendicular windows, spread southward along either side of the
river. The wide "Parade" that had shady beginnings by the Castle
became the principal street as it passed the tholsel or town hall, and
came up at length against the square old Cathedral Church of St.
Canice. The observer, confused momentarily by the medieval tor-
tuousness of the ancient town, could always locate the cathedral by
the thin column of the Irish round tower rising a clean hundred feet
over the city. Near there was the palace of the Bishop of Ossory,
Thomas Otway, who dictated the forms of prayers used at school
and on each Sunday led a procession of master and boys into the
cathedral.

The school was called Kilkenny College. Nursed by the Ormonds
from an early period, it was known in the days of Elizabeth (under a
former fellow of Oriel College, Oxford) as the best school in Ireland.
In those days it had stood "in the weste of the church-yard" of St.
Canice, but soon after the Restoration the Duke of Ormond provided
anew for it, more magnificently, on the meadows opposite his castle.
At this school Congreve spent four and a half years.

The Duke's notes give a very good idea of the building, with its

[15] The charter is printed in full by Edward Ledwich, "The History and Antiquities
of Irishtown and Kilkenny," *Collectanea de Rebus Hibernicis* (Dublin, 1781), II,
507–517.

[16] Jackson to the Duke of Ormond, 10 April 1683, Hist. MSS. Com., *Marquis of
Ormonde*, VII, N.S., 11.

[17] See a seventeenth-century painting of Kilkenny by Francis Place, reproduced by
the *Jour. of the Royal Soc. of Antiq. of Ireland* (1934), facing p. 48; also, early maps
of Kilkenny in Ledwich and in *Kilkenny Arch. Jour.* (1860–61), facing p. 35.

frontage of sixty feet and depth of eighty feet; its "good glasing of many windows"; its every story "reasonably well borded with oak boards, and strongly layed, and good strong stayrecases of oaken boards"; its first story, beginning just "a foot higher than ye kennel of ye street," for kitchen, larder, cellerage, and "eating hall"; its second story with "a very ffaire roome towards the street . . . big enough for the schoole," and other quarters for master, ushers, servants, and ten of the principal scholars; its third story "most convenient for so many schollars' chambers as it is capable off, and that can have chimneys," with "one of ye ushers . . . to regulate the schollars from disorders as may happen"; and its fourth story or garret for any overflow of students. The building would care for the master, ushers, servants, and sixty scholars—just about the number living there in Congreve's day.[18]

The novelist John Banim, a student at Kilkenny College, recalled the old building as

a gray reverend pile of irregular and rather straggling design, or we should perhaps say, of no design at all; having, partly, a monastic physiognomy, and partly that of a dwelling-house. . . . The entrance to the school-room was immediately from the street, through huge oak folding-doors, arching at top, to suit the arched stone doorway, and gained by two grand flights of steps at each side, that formed a spacious platform before the entrance, and allowed under them a passage by which visitors approached the college. To the left was another gateway, where carriages had egress. The whole front of the building was of cut stone, with Gothic windows composed of numerous small panes of glass, separately leaded, and each of diamond form; giving the appearance of a side or back rather than of a front, on account of its grotesque gables, chimneys, and spouts, the last of which jetted into the street, to the no small annoyance, in rainy weather, of the neighbors and the passengers; while, from the platform before the school-room entrance, the lads of the college contrived, in all weathers, further annoyances of every description.[19]

[18] The early history of the college is traced by Ledwich, pp. 506 ff., and by the Rev. John Browne, "Kilkenny College," *Trans. of the Kilkenny Arch. Soc.* (1850), pp. 221–229. Browne quotes the description of the school building from the manuscript notes, dated 1666, in the handwriting of the Duke of Ormond. The number of students at the school in Congreve's time is indicated by a letter from the Bishop of Ossory preserved at Kilkenny Castle. This letter, written on 18 August 1686, a few months after Congreve's withdrawal, states that unfavorable times had caused the number to drop to fifty-one.

[19] From the first chapter of the novel entitled *The Fetches*. When Banim entered Kilkenny College about 1811, apparently the old building of Congreve's period was still in use.

IV

Congreve at the age of twelve, when he entered Kilkenny, was a winsome lad. In the slight figure there was a suggestion of frailty contradicted by the firm chin and lips. Mischievous blue eyes and long brown curls set off his sensitive face. His silken waistcoat and finely knotted cravat marked him as one of gentle birth. He was a stripling, but he had poise and a lack of affectation which suggested familiarity with good society and good breeding.[20]

On his arrival at the school he was probably assigned to one of the "schollars' chambers" in the "third story." In his last year, when he had risen to the first class and was ripe for the university, he was perhaps one of the ten "principal scholars" living near the head master on the second floor. It was the death of this master's magpie which prompted Congreve to write his earliest poem of which there is any mention.[21]

During these years Congreve had two masters. The first, Dr. Henry Rider, was a Cambridge man of Trinity College. He had been brought to Ireland to head the free school in Dublin, but after some time the Duke of Ormond persuaded him to come to Kilkenny as master. This happened the year before Congreve entered. Rider was "much valued," according to the Duchess of Ormond, who went out of her way to keep him. "If upon Dean Jones's preferment," wrote the Duchess to the Earl of Arran, "there be any sinecure held by him that is in your gift I desire you will bestow it up on Mr. Ryder, the schoolmaster at Kilkenny, for his greater encouragement to continue still there; otherwise I fear without some such help he will quit that place, and then that school will break, which has hitherto had such great credit and been an advantage unto the town."[22] But clerical life called, and in spite of the Duchess Henry Ryder went back at length to Dublin and some time later became the Bishop of Killaloe.

Thus Congreve, after a year or two under Rider, came into the hands of a second master, Dr. Edward Hinton, who was installed in 1684. He was a bachelor and master of Oxford and had come to Kilkenny from the free school in Witney, Oxfordshire, where he left behind him a feeling of "good liking." For twenty years this "learned and consciencious Englishman" conducted Kilkenny College "with great industry and success."[23]

[20] Cf. the portrait of Congreve as a boy twelve years of age, facing p. 18
[21] See the article on Congreve in *Biographia Britannica*, IV (1750).
[22] See the original letters at Kilkenny Castle, dated 16 December 1682 and 6 January 1682/3. See also the entry for Henry Rider in *Alumni Cantabrigienses*.
[23] See Ledwich, p. 523; also the entry in *Alumni Oxonienses*, ed. Joseph Foster; and Anthony Wood, *Athenae Oxonienses*, IV, 478.

When Congreve enrolled at Kilkenny he was close to the average age of the sixty boys.[24] Below him were the youngsters of only nine or ten in the fifth class—the freshman group—who had been admitted after they had mastered the "accidence" elsewhere and had been fitted by this preparatory work "to enter upon grammar learning." Above him were the youths of the first class, among them Jonathan Swift, who was soon to leave for the University of Dublin.

At seven o'clock in the morning the boys assembled in the large room on the second floor for morning prayers. In the murky winter weather they sat in the schoolroom for eight hours, from seven till eleven and from one till five, well into the dusk of night. In the lengthening days of spring and summer they began their classes at six, adding another hour to the routine but ending in the pleasant late afternoon that was the gift of those happier seasons. Nine hours were none too many for the subjects of their stiff curriculum—Greek, Latin, and Hebrew, besides oratory and poetry. Religious instruction took up more time, the catechism being repeated for half an hour after morning lessons and on Sundays before the boys marched behind the master and ushers to the cathedral.

The school year bound the boys closely. Twelve whole months it ran, leaving only a few days of freedom at Easter and Whitsuntide and Christmas. Even the edge of the daily struggle was seldom softened by recess. Thursday and Saturday alone were the days to which a boy might look forward. On those days the work ended with the catechism, and the whole afternoon could be spent in following the fortunes of the rogue Guzman of Alfarache[25] or playing in the

---

[24] The ages of Kilkenny boys have been determined from the school Register. The eighteenth section of the Statutes requires "that the master shall provide a large register, wherein the names, qualities and ages of all such children as shall from time to time, be admitted into the said school, shall be registered and entered: as also the time of their departure; what class they were in, and to what place or employment they go. Likewise a catalogue of all such goods, standards and utensils, as do or shall belong to the said school-house, out-houses, garden and meadow." (Ledwich, p. 514.) The original Register begun by Dr. Edward Hinton in 1684 is preserved in the Library of Trinity College, Dublin, under the title, *The Names of such as hav[e been] Admitted into his Grace the Duke of [Ormond's] Schole in Kilkenny since Octob: 1 Ao. Dni. 1684;* also another list entitled, *The names of such as left his Grace the Duke of Ormond's Schole at Kilkenny since Octob: 1st Ao: 1684."* In the back of the Register appears a list of *The Standards belonging to his grace the Duke of Ormonds Schole in Kilkenny Octob: 1: Ao. Dni. 1684.*

[25] Aleman's *The Rogue: or, The Life of Guzman de Alfarache,* trans. by J. Mabbe (Oxford, 1630), was one of the books with Congreve's signature on the title page sold by Sotheby and Company in 1930. See *Catalogue of a Selected Portion of the Valuable Library at Hornby Castle, Bedale, Yorkshire, the Property of His Grace the Duke of Leeds*

William Congreve (Poet) as a boy

THE SCHOOLBOY AT KILKENNY

college meadow. Many years later in London Congreve recalled how he had once jumped one-and-twenty feet—an accomplishment difficult enough for a man born, as he complained, "with somewhat a round belly." At Kilkenny Congreve might also have found pleasant ways along the River Nore, which ran for five hundred yards by the side of the playing field. He could have bailed out one of the leaky boats to paddle up the river with an eye careful of the weirs, watching the flowers on the castle walls, the sprays of willows dipping to the water, and listening to the groaning of the wooden mill wheels.

But, though field and river had their attractions, Congreve probably enjoyed the indoors more. From what he says of himself, it would seem that he was nearsighted.[26] And that tells against one in open spaces. Indoors there was a little world of books. He liked the by-play of words, the joking, the relaxed association with congenial companions. Careless of the crowd, he must still have been to his chosen friends, around a can of small beer, a good companion.

Whether Congreve and Jonathan Swift began their firm friendship at this time we can only guess. Swift continued as one of the sixty boys at the school for half a year after Congreve arrived. Later another boy came who was to be, if possible, a warmer friend of Congreve's throughout life. This was Joseph Keally, eldest son of a country family with its seat at Keally Mount, some miles outside of Kilkenny. Later at the law courts in London these two were inseparable companions. And even after Keally returned to Ireland to practice law, Congreve wrote to him steadfastly and awaited eagerly Keally's comings to London. They had similar bents—loved books, made translations, and dabbled in politics. They both ate and drank too much, and Keally did not fight against fatness with even the middling success of Congreve. Before he died at forty, Keally had grown so stout that an extra team of horses was regularly hitched to his carriage to pull him up the hill to Keally Mount.[27] Writing to

---

(London, 1930), Lot 9. The signature "Will: Congreve," in Congreve's own hand-writing, was that regularly used by the young Congreve. In later years he used "W." or "Wm." or "William."

[26] See Letter XLIX, to Edward Porter, in which Congreve speaks of "a whole river in cascade falling so near me that even I can distinctly see it." This letter was written in his twenty-second year, long before he had the trouble with cataracts that required treatment by a French surgeon.

[27] The fame of Keally's obesity is still current in Ireland in the neighborhood of Keally Mount, as I have been informed by Miss Kathleen Lynch. For information regarding Joseph Keally see the Register of Kilkenny College; *Alumni Oxonienses;* *Middle Temple, Admissions to House & Chambers,* 1658–1695 (Manuscript in the Library of the Middle Temple); G. D. Burtchaell, *Genealogical Memoirs of the Members*

Keally, Congreve once spoke with compassionate understanding of "our fat friends" and his own "round belly." Those Kilkenny evenings were very pleasant, but they brought their after-affects years later in enforced visits to Epsom or Tunbridge, in Congreve's writing Keally to meet him at the Bath, in his acquiring a physique almost feminine in its weakness.

Congreve had no great amount of physical energy; he loved his ease. But he also loved his books, and at least a gentlemanly amount of real study. For Greek he developed a genuine feeling. His Master Hinton had demonstrated a scholarly interest in the language by publishing, before he came to Kilkenny, a translation from the Greek of Plutarch entitled "The Apophthegms or remarkable sayings of Kings and great Commanders." Under Hinton's influence and guidance Congreve began to make of himself the Greek scholar whom Dryden was later to pronounce "more capable than any man" of translating Homer.

V

In the air at Kilkenny there were dramatic memories, running back a hundred and thirty years to the days when John Bale from the bishop's palace gave his plays in the town streets, to the time when "the yonge men, in the forenoon, played a tragedye of God's promyses in the olde law, at the Market Cross, with organe plainges and songes very aptly," and in the afternoon "a comedie of Sanct Johan Baptistes preaching of Christe's baptisynge, and of his temptacion in the wildernesse."[28] In that day, too, the boys at Kilkenny produced miracle plays of their own which pleased the Bishop and made him praise their acting skill.

The city officers, mayor and aldermen, had continued through the years to encourage the players. They gave the necessary trappings for miracle plays and interludes almost down to Congreve's day.[29] As late as the middle of the seventeenth century the city treasury paid for music, for feeding the actors, for "placing the Stacions," for "six paire of Gloves for Christe, John Evangeliste, Mary Mother, and the three other Maryes."

---

of Parliament for the County and City of Kilkenny (Dublin, 1888); and Kathleen M. Lynch, "Congreve's Irish Friend, Joseph Keally," *PMLA*, LIII (1938), 1076–87.

[28] Bayle's comment, as quoted by John G. A. Prim, "Olden Popular Pastimes in Kilkenny," *Kilkenny Arch. Jour.*, II (1852–53), 327.

[29] Numerous references to such plays in the Kilkenny Corporations Records, preserved in the Town Hall, are quoted and discussed by Prim. During the period when the London theatres were closed by act of Parliament, *A Tragedy of Cola's Furie, or Lirenda's Miserie*, by Henry Burkhead, was printed at Kilkenny, 1645. The names of the actors on the back of the title leaf indicate that the play was actually produced.

The mayor and aldermen went so far as to pay the schoolmaster for teaching the children their parts. They paid the chief actors, a certain Thomas Lucas getting three shillings and four pence "for his paynes for rendering the part Charlemayne"; and Simon Archer, ten pence "for playing a conqueror upon Midsummer Eve." Thus they branched off from the miracles into the intermediate folk plays and romantic medleys.

The work of the local players was supplemented now and then by professional companies from Dublin. Joseph Ashbury and his Smock Alley troopers came down to entertain the Duke of Ormond and his court. These performances and amateur plays acted at Kilkenny College could scarcely have been lost upon Congreve. Indeed, there is every reason to believe that before Dr. Hinton wrote into his register, "William Congreve of the first Class Entered the University of Dublin, April Ao. 1686," that youth had already become a student of the stage.

CHAPTER III

TRINITY COLLEGE AND SMOCK ALLEY

I

FOR Kilkenny boys desirous of a larger world the road led north to Dublin. And so Congreve went up to college not by any means a stranger. A few of his schoolfellows had broken from scholarship. John Walker was mixing salves for a Dublin chirurgeon, and Godfrey Burden was doing prentice work for a merchant.[1] But most of the Kilkennians passed straight from the meadows of Kilkenny to the meadows of Trinity College. One of these was a handsome boy with black eyebrows who nourished a hatred of mathematics. His name was Jonathan Swift.

School and college were closely bound together. The Duke of Ormond, patron of Kilkenny, was also Chancellor of Trinity. For one he selected the Master and for the other the Provost. And the Provost of Trinity College was always one of three visitors to supervise and direct the Duke's school at Kilkenny. At least one day each year Provost Huntington appeared pontifically before Congreve and his fellows. Naturally, Kilkennians continued their studies at Trinity. In the year that Congreve came up, he together with his schoolfellows made up an eighth of the Trinity freshman class.

The Duke had an idea of maintaining among the Kilkenny boys a group of selected "Ormond Scholars," to be trained expressly for Trinity College. But Congreve would hardly have been an Ormond Scholar. He had little initiative, little desire to push himself. He was happy when inconspicuous. He did not readily follow the strict routine that would please the master.

In the spring of 1686 Congreve found Trinity College a minuscule world of quadrangles and courts set on the southern bank of the River Liffey. To the west "College Green" led into a city rapidly changing from medieval gray to Queen Anne red brick. To the south the college gardens and the Provost's orchard stretched out to St. Stephen's Green. To the east broad meadows ran out along the bay and the open sea.

---

[1] For the names of students who had gone up to Dublin before Congreve, see the Trinity College MS. entitled *The Names of such as left his Grace the Duke of Ormond's Schole at Kilkenny since Octob: 1st: Ao: 1684.*

The "Old Quadrangle" was the largest.[2] The smell of roast beef from the commons called to dinner. The odor of leather bindings in the library called to study amid a substantial collection of books and seven hundred famous manuscripts that had been assembled by Primate Usher and the Countess of Bath or else ravished in Elizabeth's day from the libraries of Spain. The Provost lodged in this quadrangle, and at one corner it was joined to the school chapel. Smaller, newer buildings had been erected outside by Sir Jerome Alexander. There were playing fields, gardens, and lush Irish grass in plenty all around, and far off the green and blue shimmer of the occasionally sun-lit Wicklow Hills.

Along with Dr. Hinton's son, John, and two other Kilkennians, Congreve matriculated on Monday, the fifth of April.[3] He was characteristically tardy. Hinton presented himself to the Senior Lecturer at seven in the morning, but Congreve did not appear until what was for the seventeenth century the late hour of ten. It may be noted that Hinton went on to win a scholarship at college.

Hinton also got his name down first in the Buttery Book[4]—a weekly list of all students, with records of purchases and class attendance—while Congreve got in last of all the Kilkennians. He only managed to get his name put down between lines and was carelessly

[2] The equipment, the appearance, and the general plan of Trinity College in Congreve's day are clearly set forth by the descriptions and pen sketches of Thomas Dingley in his *Observations*, pp. 1–75.

[3] Congreve's matriculation is recorded as follows: "1685. Die quinto Aprillis. Hora deci, promeri. Pupillus: Gulielmus Congreve. Pensio. Parens: filius Guli: Congreve, Generosi de Yogholia. Aetas: annos natus Sexdecim. Ubi Natus: Natus Bardsagranus in Com. Eboracen: Aus: b. 5. Ubi Educatus: Educatus Kilkeniae Sub feru. Doctris Hinton. Tutor: St. Geo: Ashe L. K. 4." This entry is copied from *Catalogus omnium Studentium admissox in Collegium SSce. et individuae Trinitatis ex fundatione Serenissimae Reginae Elizabethae juxta Dublin, ab anno 1637, mense Januario feliciter incepit*, T. C. D. MS., Registrar's Office. The manuscript is a nineteenth century copy of the original register, which is now lost. An eighteenth century abstract of the original, preserved at the Herald's Office, Dublin, I have been able to consult through the kindness of T. U. Sadleir, Esq. Both the abstract and the *Catalogus* give the year as 1685, referring to the Trinity College year, which began 9 July 1685 and ended 8 July 1686.

[4] The materials in this chapter are drawn largely from manuscripts preserved at Trinity College and at the National Library of Ireland, especially from the minutes of the Provost and Fellows of Trinity College (*General Registry from 1640 to 1740*) and from the Buttery Book for 1685–1687. These minutes and the Buttery Book, interpreted in the light of the voluminous statutes under which the college was operating, give much information about the college and the individual students. For the statutes see *Charta sive Literae Patentes, a Serenissimo Rege Carolo Primo Collegio Sanctae & Individuae Trinitatis juxta Dublin, Concessa. Una cum Statutis ejusdem Collegii*. Dublinii: MDCCXXV.

designated as "Jho" Congreve. The Buttery clerk continued for
several weeks to be baffled by that first name, probably because Congreve was reticent or—like Charles Lamb—blubbery in pronuncia-
tion.

Congreve soon found himself clad in a black and sombre gown, sitting at mealtime with three hundred other students in the large Hall
and chatting in Latin. He came under the rule of Provost Huntington
and the sixteen Fellows. More particularly he found himself one of the
middle register of the college social life. He belonged, after paying on
entrance eight pounds of "caution money," to the class of students
known as Pensioners.

Above in the top of the social register swaggered the few Fellow
Commoners, who, by paying double fees, were given special privileges.
Among other things they were excused from tipping their caps to the
Fellows. In the depths labored the thirty Sizars, bearing all indignities
and no honors. They were poor boys. They paid but little money and
worked about the school, waiting on tables and marking class rolls.

As one of the middle group Congreve paid the regular tuition of
forty shillings. His other fees ran thus:

> To the Senior Lecturer, 5 shillings.
> To the Butler, 2 shillings.
> To the Clerk of ye Buttery, 1 shilling.
> To the Cook, 2 shillings.
> To the Manciple, 1 shilling.
> To the Porter, 1 shilling.
> To the Provost's Sizar, 1 shilling.
> To the College for a spoon, 12 shillings.

Congreve roomed in the Old Quadrangle near his tutor, St. George
Ashe. Had he come to Trinity a generation earlier, the two would
probably have slept in the same room. The relation between student
and tutor was still very intimate. St. George Ashe not only taught and
advised him but was his overseer under the Provost, an intermediary
receiving his tuition and his absence fines, and his money laid out for
beer and wines from the cellar.

This tutor was a follower of Euclid, a stargazer, a member of the
Royal Society. It was for his research that Trinity had purchased its
mathematical instruments. Twenty-eight years old, seven of these
spent at Trinity, he was already a ripe scholar. Yet, in spite of the
time he took for geometry and papers for the *Philosophical Transactions* of the Royal Society, he saw much of his students and stood
higher in Trinity hearts than any of the other Fellows. Not long after
Congreve left Trinity, Ashe was made its Provost and then later was

given a bishopric. When he died in 1718 Addison felt that he had "scarce left behind him his equal in humanity, agreeable conversation, and all kinds of learning." "Never a Bishop in England," chimed in Swift, "with half the wit of St. George Ashe."[5]

As can be imagined, Congreve was always on hand for the mathematics lectures given by his congenial tutor, though Swift, despite the splendid mathematical instruments, was notoriously absent. He already cherished that keen hatred which, forty years after, was to break out in the satirical thrusts of Gulliver's voyage to Laputa. As for his science lectures, however, Congreve was a shirker. The meeting hour of six o'clock, the time of thin dawn and sticky eyes, must have had a lot to do with that. In Greek he carried on as at Kilkenny, full of the zeal and punctuality established in him by his former master, Dr. Hinton. In his first year, according to the exact record of the Buttery Book, he missed only one Greek lecture.

Congreve held fast to the Greek poets, but otherwise seems to have drowsed his way through Trinity studies. His former schoolmate John Hinton was making headway toward one of the fifty-eight Scholarships. Congreve never arrived there, impeded perhaps by his faltering way of speaking, by his shyness, but most likely by his laziness and shirking of college work.

He ate enormously, never once missing commons, repeatedly ordering up "sizings," additional food from the kitchen. He drained the Trinity cellar of much of its beer and wine; he bought of the buttery clerk just six times as many mugs and glasses as frugal Swift. In later London life Swift wrote Stella of winey evenings passed with Congreve. Most likely the wine had begun flowing first in Congreve's room in the old Trinity Quad, with Congreve the host then as he was later in London. The lukewarm relationship between scholarship and Madeira may be exemplified by the fact that Hinton made no demands on the Trinity cellar.

Besides fat living, Dublin, and especially the Dublin evenings, may have beckoned. Life at Trinity was cramped and tedious; its gates, shut after supper, were guarded by a gowned porter. One boy named Spencer had to confess on his knees in the great hall for wounding the porter in a tussle. Another named Mosse was brought before the Provost for tampering with the gate locks. Still the students kept escaping over the walls into the night life of Dublin until

[5] Swift's *Correspondence*, ed. Elrington Ball, 6 vols. (London 1910–14), III, 3; I, 182; see also the account of St. George Ashe in *DNB*. The manuscript minutes of the meetings of Provost and Fellows of Trinity College for the period following 1679 have many references to Congreve's tutor.

finally during Congreve's last year the Fellows ordered "that the
walls of the college be built three foot higher."[6] If one did get over
the wall, it meant a riotous time. Beyond the College Green lay a
world of taverns. Neile Duncan was dismissed from Trinity for bilk-
ing a tavern and fighting. Others were haled before the Provost for
raising a tumult in the town. And Swift was up, too, for "notorious
neglect of duties, and frequenting the town."[7]

II

But beyond these, one deeper interest held Congreve from his studies. Of this the Buttery Book of Trinity tells the best story. For,
while according to it Congreve repeatedly missed six o'clock chapel
—a natural thing for one who was to protest in *The Old Bachelor*
against vulgar early rising—there are other absences not so obviously
explained. These are the absences from the study of the catechism on
Saturday afternoons. These do not, as might be first thought, reflect
a want of appetite for Anglican liturgy. Instead they suggest that
something more important to William was occurring at the same
time. While John Hinton and others were listening dutifully to the
chaplain, Congreve was absent—perhaps a mile away in Dublin,
waiting for the curtain to go up on the stage of the Smock Alley theatre and for the faces of Joseph Ashbury and his comedians to appear.

On Saturday afternoon stage and studies conflicted. Presumably
Congreve chose the stage, nor was he the first Trinity man to do so.
As early as 1630 the Senior Sophisters were acting a comedy and the
Bachelors a play. Their dramatic work went on, gaining support from
the town to such a degree that the Deputies of Dublin Castle stepped
in and forced the Provost against his will to allow the students to act
their play. The appearance of a professional company so excited the
students that the Archbishop of Dublin was moved to lament their
loving the stage better than their studies.[8]

In Dublin by 1636 the common players of interludes were so nois-
ily obtrusive that the Irish Parliament began to legislate against them.
Thereupon the Lord Deputy, by making John Ogilby Master of Revels in Ireland, did his best to reform and bring order to Dublin theat-
ricals.[9] Ogilby began his task by erecting "at his own great cost and

[6] *Registry*, 19 July 1688.

[7] *Registry*, 18 March 1686/7.

[8] For the early interest of the students in dramatic productions see John William
Stubbs, *The History of the University of Dublin* (Dublin, 1889), p. 63; J. T. Gilbert,
A History of the City of Dublin, 3 vols. (Dublin, 1854–59), II, 70.

[9] For the history of the professional theatre in Dublin before the Restoration see
LaTourette Stockwell, "New Light on the Werburgh Street Theatre," Dublin Maga-

charges. . .a public theatre in. . . Dublin." This was the only play-house of the British Isles outside of London before the Restoration. And it was in Dublin alone, outside of London, that distinguished companies of professional actors were encouraged and supported during the seventeenth century. This Irish theatre was sponsored by James Shirley, the dramatist, and there his own plays as well as those of Jonson and Middleton and others were produced before the gentlefolk.

The word *gentlefolk* is the right one, for the Dublin theatre had sprung up between the theatrical activity of Elizabeth's day and that of Charles II, and looked not toward the past but toward the aristocratic future, when the *London Gazette* for 5-9 January 1670/71, reporting affairs in Dublin, would speak of "most of the Nobility and Gentry being at a Play, at the Publick Play-house." James Shirley, like Etherege later in London, pointed his plays for the ladies and gentlemen of the court circle. The atmosphere of the theatre was Restoration.

In Ireland, as in England, the theatre was cheered by the return of Charles II. Ogilby was given the royal patent for the Revels of Ireland.[10] The old playhouse being in ruins, he built afresh in Smock Alley, a pinched old street lying between the Castle and the Liffey, scarce a mile from Trinity College. With pit and boxes and two galleries, it was like the London theatres, and of it Katherine Philips, the "Matchless Orinda," wrote in 1662, "We have a new Playhouse here, which in my opinion is much finer than D'Avenant's."[11] Such was the first of the famous Smock Alley theatres. A Londoner noted that the actors were in "no way inferior to those in London" and that the spectators were not "one degree less in Vanity and fopperie."[12]

Great actors were to take their turns upon the Smock Alley boards, among them Wilks and Booth, Macklin and Garrick. In Congreve's

zine, VII (1932), No. 4, pp. 33–40; LaTourette Stockwell, *Dublin Theatres and Theatre Customs* (Kingsport Press, 1938).

[10] Ogilby was granted the patent on 8 May 1661. On 5 April 1663, Ogilby and Thomas Stanley were granted a patent jointly, "With power to build one or more theatres in Dublin or elsewhere, upon such ground as Mr. Ogilby should purchase in fee." Ogilby died in 1676. Stanley surrendered his patent on 19 November 1683, and on 11 August 1684 the patent was granted to William Morgan, Joseph Ashbury, and Charles Ashbury (son of Joseph) during their lives. On 9 April 1719, Morgan and Charles Ashbury being dead, Anthony Twyman was granted the reversion of the patent on the death of Joseph Ashbury. See *Liber Munerum Publicorum Hiberniae* (1824), I, Part II, p. 93.

[11] See W. J. Lawrence, "Irish Players at Oxford in 1677," *The Elizabethan Playhouse and Other Studies*, Second Series (Stratford-upon-Avon, 1913), p. 194.

[12] John Dunton's manuscript notes on Ireland, Bodleian MS. Rawl. D. 71, f. 25.

day the Dublin stage was directed by a player who was perhaps, close to the young dramatist himself. This was Joseph Ashbury, a man but a year younger than Congreve's father and like him a lieutenant in the Irish regiment of the Duke of Ormond.[13] Joseph Ashbury may have been a close friend of the Congreve family, and it is pleasant to imagine that he was the tutor of William Congreve in the ways of the stage.

Ashbury acted well and taught well. During half a century he sent across to England, Wilks, Booth, Doggett, Norris, and Quin to live forever in the memories of English playgoers. Occasionally he took his company to England, as when in 1677 he performed for three weeks in Oxford. His troupers came to know Congreve and later they bobbed up in Congreve's way in London. Richard Estcourt founded the Beefsteak Club in London and laughed over many a glass of wine with Congreve and Swift. Trefusis reappeared, summons in hand, as the original Trapland in *Love for Love*. Bowen appeared as Sir Joseph Wittol in *The Old Bachelor*, played slyly as Jeremy in *Love for Love*, and was the foolish Witwoud of *The Way of the World*. Thomas Doggett, the old dotard husband in *The Old Bachelor*, became gloriously famous as Sailor Ben in *Love for Love*. He was still Congreve's good friend at the time of his death in 1721.[14]

Besides hobnobbing with actors and watching the comedies of Etherege and Wycherley and Shadwell, Congreve read about dramatic technique. He bought three books on the subject, all in the editions of 1684. These were Roscommon's translation of Horace's *Ars Poetica*, Dryden's *Essay of Dramatic Poesy*, and the two volumes of François Hadelin's *Whole Art of the Stage*.[15] That he read them to some effect is shown by his calling attention to observance of the dramatic unities in his own novel, written, it is said, during his college days. In the preface to this novel he blazes out: "All Traditions must indisputably give place to the *Drama*."

---

[13] Although Joseph Ashbury's joint patent as Master of the Revels for Ireland was not granted till 1684, he had been active in the Dublin theatre for perhaps ten or fifteen years before. In a list of "The King's Guard of Horse," Dublin, of about 1677, he is mentioned as a "Comedian," thirty years of age, who had entered the Guard in 1667. See Hist. MSS. Com., *Report on the Manuscripts of the Marquis of Ormonde* (London, 1899), II, 237. See also the account of Joseph Ashbury in *DNB*.

[14] Of the actors named, Estcourt, Bowen, and Trefusis were still in Dublin for the opening of the theatre after the Revolution. See Gilbert, *A History of the City of Dublin*, II, 69.

[15] These four volumes, with Congreve's name on each title page, were listed by Sotheby and Company, 1930, among books to be sold from the library of the Duke of Leeds, Lots 209 and 298.

III

If Congreve, on entering college in April of 1686, had cared to cast his eyes over the political scene, he might have noted the preliminary stirrings of events that would in time swirl him in their backwater from Ireland to England. It was the period of James II in England, and James II was enforcing his Catholic program. This came home to the Congreves when the Earl of Tyrconnel was sent fresh from England, determined to hunt Protestants out of the army. It went hard with Lieutenant Congreve as an Anglican officer. A fellow officer lost outright a commission costing sixteen hundred pounds. One after another the Anglican names fell from the rolls.

A student in Trinity might have been deceived by the quiet of the library. But beyond the walls, out in the town, muskets were being cocked and pikes swung. In time, running together with English events, the conflict grew more visible until Catholics were seizing the maces of all corporations and Tyrconnel's army was stealing and plundering.

Fear grew intense. The College plate was locked in a strong box. The college pension was discontinued. Apprehension grew steadily through 1687 and 1688. Some whispered of another St. Bartholomew. The decks of ships were crowded with fleeing Anglicans, and horsemen were delayed at smithies while heavy fingers tempered war steel.

While William of Orange was disembarking at Torbay, the college was pleading with tenants to pay. In a year the usual sixty or eighty new students had dropped to a mere thirteen. The college stock had fallen so low that even these could not be properly fed. Early in 1689 manuscripts and plate were sent to England. And in February a bit of kindness was shown as two hundred pounds went to England "for the support of those Fellows that should be forc't to fly thither." "At the same time," continues the Registry, "the dangers of staying in the College seemed so great that it was judg'd reasonable that all those that thought fit to withdraw themselves from the College for their better security might have free liberty so to do."

Late in the same month Tyrconnel's soldiers were poking with their muskets through the rooms of the College. St. George Ashe and four other Fellows sailed in March. Congreve too found his way to England, though the exact time is unknown. By September Trinity College was closed. The ancient owl of wisdom perched desolate on the steep slate roof of the Old Quadrangle, and Anglican prisoners sat gloomily in the yard.

CHAPTER IV

THE LITERARY MIDDLE TEMPLAR

I

MONTHS before Trinity College closed its doors in Dublin, Congreve's father was listed as one of "such protestant officers as have been lately in the army in Ireland, and are now out of employment in and about London, and desire to be entertained in His Majesty's service."[1] But young Congreve, on leaving college, did not immediately join his father. His way to London led through Staffordshire, where his grandfather Richard was lord of Stretton Manor. There in Staffordshire the nineteen-year-old boy tarried during the spring and summer of 1689.

Stretton Manor is said to have been built early in the seventeenth century by the great architect Inigo Jones. It was a pleasant vacation place, with silvery lake and cool lawns. Under one of the old oaks, tradition says, Congreve penned the first draft of *The Old Bachelor*. And tradition is supported by Congreve's insistence that he wrote the play before going up to London later in the year.

In Staffordshire the young man met Katherine Leveson. She was the daughter of Robert Leveson, who had been Justice of Peace for the county along with Congreve's grandfather.[2] Katherine's brother Richard was already an officer in the army, Member of Parliament for Lichfield, and Groom of the King's Bedchamber. Ten years older than Congreve and matured by her contacts in London, Katherine might easily have taken the fancy of an impressionable lad fresh from Ireland—might even have left her mark, however lightly, upon the first draft of *The Old Bachelor*. Assuming that Congreve drew from life, we might suppose that Katherine Leveson contributed something to the conception of Araminta, just as Anne Bracegirdle more certainly influenced the heroines of the later comedies. In dedicating his

[1] B. M. Add. MSS. 28,938, f. 314.

[2] Katherine Leveson was the second of six children, as shown by *Staffordshire Pedigrees based on the Visitation of that County made by William Dugdale Esquire, Norroy King of Arms, in the years 1663–1664, from the original manuscript written by Gregory King . . . during the years 1680 to 1700*, ed. Sir George J. Armytage, Bart., and W. H. Rylands; Publ. of Harl. Soc., LXIII (London, 1912), pp. 156, 157. See also *Collections*, William Salt Arch. Soc. (1920), pp. 129, 157.

youthful novel to Mrs. Katherine Leveson two years later, Congreve recalled her "Skill," her "Clear Wit," and her "sound Judgment," and he took pride in calling himself her "Friend."

Congreve was in Staffordshire during the last months of his grandfather's life. On the 11th of June, 1689, the eighty-year-old Richard Congreve of Stretton Hall signed his last will and testament.[3]

Sick and weake of body but of sound . . . minde . . . my body . . . to be decently buried in the Chancell of the Church at Stretton betwxt the bodies of my dearest wife and my daughter Martha. . . . I give and bequeath unto my son William Congreve the sume of One hundred pounds to be paid him by the heirs, Execs: or Adms: of my late son John Congreve within six months after my decease being part of the fower hundred pounds I was to receive for the Wood.

Then follow definite bequests to be paid out of his "usuall Estate":

To his daughter Francis Holt, £100.
To his grandchildren Elizabeth and Carola Newth, £20 each.
To his faithful servant Jane Hart and to his grandchildren Frances Holt and Thomas Gaywood, the remainder of his usual estate—the three sharing equally.

He made Thomas Gaywood sole executor of his will, and signed it in a clear, firm hand, "Ric: Congreve."

In the middle of August, 1689, the old grandfather died. Perhaps his son the Lieutenant, down from London, stood with young William in the chapel near the manor house on the 19th of August when Richard Congreve was "decently buried" in the chancel at Stretton between young William's grandmother and Aunt Martha. Since Richard Congreve's oldest son John was already dead, the estate passed by English law of entail to the grandson John. Some idea of Stretton Hall is given by "A true and pfect Inventory of all and singular ye goods household stuffe Cattle and Chattells of Richard Congreve late of Stretton in the County of Stafford Esq decd taken and Apprized 29 Aug: 1689." The twenty-one divisions of this inventory, and some of the items, are listed below.

1) 6 oxen £22
   12 cows £28
   22 "younge beests" £27
   9 swine £7-13-4
   Barley £20

[3] Proved 19 March 1689/90, Lichfield Peculiar Court, Birmingham. Attached to this will, and dated 29 August 1689, is an interesting inventory of "ye goods household stuffe Cattle and Chattells of Richard Congreve late of Stretton." The burial of Richard Congreve is recorded in the Stretton Church Register.

Peas £8

Hay £20

Oats £3-10

Horses, Mares and Colts £34

"One cutting knife" 1s. 6d.

2) "Goodes" in the Kitchen
18 pewter dishes, etc. £3-1-0

3) "Goodes" in Cheese Chamber

4) "Goodes" in Dark Closet

5) "Goodes" in Lower Closet

6) In the Hall
1 long table £3
2 short tables 13s.
3 chairs 4s.
1 clock £1-10-0
1 screen and a folding screen 3s. 6d.
2 brass candlesticks 2s. 6d.

7) In the Great Parlor (about £4½)
Tables, chairs—also one looking glass at £1

8) In the Little Parlor

9) "Goodes" in several Butteries £2-5

10) "In the closet Bookes of all sorts prospective glasses . . . dyalls and other thyngs at . . . £10-0-0"

11) In Closet Chamber.

12) In Chamber over Parlor £5-15

13) In the Maid's Chamber

14) In the Gallery—old trunk, etc.

15) Over the Hall—2 bedsteads at 10s.

16) In the Further Stone Chamber

17) In the Great Parlor Chamber

18) Over the Gate House—beds, tables, chairs, etc. £1-12

19) Servant Man's Chamber

20) In Stable—saddles, bridles, etc. 15s.

21) Goods not before Appraised—£1

Total £300

Appraised by Willm Southall, H. Hickins, Geo. Whitridge, John Byrch, Geo. Malkin.

The one hundred pounds willed to Lieutenant Congreve was enough to support his little family in London until, in July of the following year, he got another commission in the army. The new appointment was in the Earl of Danby's volunteer regiment.[4] In the summer of 1690 most of the regular English troops had accompanied William III to Ireland. Then came word of the victory of the French

---

[4] P. R. O., Military Entry Book 2, p. 145.

fleet over the English and Dutch fleets off Beachy Head. England seemed to be at the mercy of the French. So the Earl of Danby hastily formed a volunteer regiment of dragoons, in which he gave the former Lieutenant William Congreve a commission as captain. But the French did not follow up their victory over the English, did not attempt to invade England, and the services of Danby's volunteers were not long required. Again out of employment, Captain Congreve turned his thoughts toward Ireland and in October, 1690, sailed from Bristol[5] to become chief agent for the Irish estates of Richard Boyle, Earl of Cork and Burlington.

II

Left behind, young William was by no means a stranger in London. Among other acquaintances he found there a number of his Staffordshire and Yorkshire cousins. Ralph Congreve, a year older than he, had just become an ensign. In good time he attained the rank of colonel and commanded the key fortifications of Gibraltar. He made his London home in Clarges Street, in the fashionable suburb of Westminister.

Ralph Congreve's younger brother William[6] was also in and about London, beginning a long military career. Commissioned lieutenant as early as 1690, he later became colonel and resided in the London suburb of Highgate. Colonel William Congreve of Highgate was only a year younger than our William Congreve the dramatist, and the two were sometimes confused, even in their own time. On one occasion the Bank of England credited to the dramatist's account some two hundred pounds belonging to the colonel.[7] Today the confusion of these two Congreves has become more common through the sale of many documents signed by one of the two and usually attributed to the dramatist. Not a few libraries have added to the confusion by classifying under the name of the dramatist the manuscripts of both men. Fortunately the resulting errors can be corrected, with a little care, by a study of the known handwriting and signatures of the dramatist. A convenient key is furnished by a document signed by both men as joint executors for the will of Ralph Congreve.[8]

[5] P. R. O., S. P. Dom., Warrant Book 35, p. 408.

[6] For information regarding Ralph and William Congreve (the poet's cousins) see the Congreve family papers at the William Salt Library, Stafford; the *Erdswick Book* now in the possession of Sir Geoffrey Congreve, Bart., Chartley Hall, Staffordshire; and the will of Ralph Congreve, dated 6 November 1725, proved 3 December 1725, P. C. C., Romney 247, Somerset House.

[7] See Bank of England, Folio 139. The error was made 26 June 1719 and corrected 22 December 1719.   [8] Dated 26 February 1725/26, Harvard Theatre Collection.

Besides his cousins Ralph and William, Congreve had in London other relatives on his father's side. While he was still in Ireland his Aunt Carola had married a Londoner, and after he arrived in London another Staffordshire kinswoman married Humphry Morice, later Governor of the Bank of England.

More prominent in London were Congreve's Yorkshire cousins, kinsmen on his mother's side. As we have already noticed, the two daughters of Sir John Lewis—the cousin on whose estate Congreve was born—had married into the nobility. The older daughter was the wife of Theophilus, seventh Earl of Huntingdon, who had his town house in Westminster not far from Congreve's lodgings in the Strand. The Earl's daughter, Lady Elizabeth Hastings,[9] became celebrated for her beauty and ideal life. "To love her," wrote Steele, " is a liberal education." Congreve also praised her "unaffected charms" and her mind, "the Seat of Honour, Truth, Compassion, Knowledge, and Innocence."[10] Sir John's younger daughter had married Robert Leke, third Earl of Scarsdale, whose town residence was in Duke Street. Congreve came to know him all too well, for Robert Leke was later the poet's rival for the affections of Anne Bracegirdle. Before Congreve came up to London, Sir John Lewis had died at Ledstone Park. His widow married Denzil Onslow and was living in London as late as 1694.

The prominence of these family connections in London made it easy for Congreve to claim the high social position for which he was eminently fitted by his wit and his training.

III

By the spring of 1691 William Congreve the elder was well enough established in his Irish post to enter his son as a student of the law.[11] Young Congreve now began to come into his own—in the pleasant walks and under the arches of the Middle Temple, where great law-

---

[9] See the accounts of Theophilus Hastings, seventh Earl of Huntingdon, and of Lady Elizabeth Hastings in *DNB;* also the Report of the Hist. MSS. Com. on the MSS. of Reginald Rawson Hastings, Esq., I (1928), II (1930).

[10] *The Tatler,* No. 42. Steele's eulogy came later in *The Tatler,* No. 49.

[11] From the Register of the Middle Temple: "Martii 17 1690 [1691]. Mr. Wilmus Congreve, filius et heres apparens Wilm: Congreve de Stretton in Com Staffordiae, Ar: admissus est in Societatem Medii Templi specialiter et obligatur unacum et dat pro fine . . . 05 = 00 = 00." This statement about the father is a means of identification rather than an indication that the older Congreve was actually in Stretton at the time. Perhaps his place of residence in Ireland since his recent return was not yet fixed. He had sailed from Bristol to Ireland in October, 1690, and was giving advice to the Council at Youghal on 19 September 1691. See *The Council Book of the Corporation of Youghal,* ed. Richard Caulfield (Guildford, Surrey, 1878), pp. 386–387.

yers and true poets had mused during many a century. In Shakespeare's lifetime the barristers had seen *Twelfth Night* played within their stately hall. But the Temple was then a place for serious study of the law, with readers appointed by the benchers, or senior members, to direct the "barristers," and with many moot courts. During the seventeenth century, however, the "readings" and the "mootings" were almost discontinued; and by the time Congreve went into residence in 1691, the routine of the Middle Temple was not one to disturb the pursuit of belles-lettres. On the contrary, Congreve found that the Inns of Court had recently nursed the three comic dramatists of the Restoration whose writings most nearly pointed the way toward his own comedies: Etherege, who had inaugurated the comedy of manners and had capped his work with the brilliant inanities of Sir Fopling Flutter; Wycherley, whose *Plain Dealer* was strong medicine even for the Restoration; and Shadwell, still in his prime, with such recent successes as *The Squire of Alsatia* and *Bury Fair*.

This literary tradition suited Congreve's mood. The law was not for him. Although he continued for three or four years in the "Society of the Middle Temple," he made but little progress toward the bar. Like Steele's literary Templar, described twenty years later in the second number of *The Spectator*, he had "chosen his Place of Residence rather to obey the Direction of an old humorsom Father, than in pursuit of his own Inclinations. He was placed there to study the Laws of the Land, and is the most learned of any of the House in those of the Stage."

With genial fellows—young men like Walter Moyle just up from Oxford—more interested in Drury Lane than in chancery suits, it is not surprising that Congreve found himself at the playhouse or at Will's more frequently than at Westminster Hall. The Middle Temple, adjoining Fleet Street, was but a short distance from the Theatre Royal in Drury Lane, the only place in London at which plays had been given regularly since the two dramatic companies had united in 1682. And Will's Coffeehouse, rendezvous of the Wits, was in the neighborhood of the theatre in the direction of Covent Garden. Congreve, like Steele's Templar, must frequently have taken a turn there before going to the play; and afterwards, of course, it was necessary to join the critics at the coffeehouse. Much later Steele recalled with enthusiasm the "old times" when it had been the custom "to sit upon a play" at Will's "after it was acted."

Congreve's early years in London found the literary society at Will's at its best. Pepys had enjoyed its "very witty and pleasant discourse." By the last decade of the century Dryden was the unchallenged prince of critics and writers, and he held his court at Will's. Dryden's disciples were so numerous that Will Urwin, the owner, would have been wealthy but for the proverbial empty pockets of the Wits. As Jeremy remarks in *Love for Love*, "The Man of the House would have been an Alderman by this time with half the Trade, if he had set up in the City."

Congreve sat, like Mirabel, pipe in hand, at the long tables in Will's. There he observed Petulant rushing out to page himself or to answer a call from the ladies in the coach; and Sir Willful Witwoud, just up from the country on his travels to show that England has "Blockheads of all Ages." How he enjoyed all this! He comments delightedly on these "Strange Animals" in writing to his fellow Templar and crony at Will's—young Walter Moyle, who had gone down into his native Cornwall to win a seat in Parliament. "It had been much to the Disadvantage of *Pliny*," Congreve continues, "had the *Coffee-house* been in his Days; for sure he would have described some who frequent it; which would have given him, the Reputation of a more fabulous Writer than he has now. But being in our Age it does him a Service, for we who know it, can give Faith to all his Monsters."[12] And yet this Congreve, who cold detach himself from the bickerings of the Stuart drawing room, who could step back and look at valet, master, and father—at Jeremy, Valentine, and Sir Sampson —was not a cold spectator at the hearth. For a few years he threw himself merrily into the life of the coffeehouse clubs, the "Grave-Club" and the "Rabble," as he calls them.

But Congreve also enjoyed getting "out of the world" to some place where "nothing but the last great news could have reached." Such a place was Dovedale among the mountains of Derbyshire, from which he wrote during the last half of 1692:

I have a little tried what Solitude and retirement can afford, which are here in perfection. I am now writing to you from before a black mountain nodding over me and a whole river in Cascade falling so near me that even I can distinctly see it. I can only tell you of the situation I am in which would be better express'd by Mr Grace if he were here.

Perhaps the mood of this quiet mountain retreat is reflected in Congreve's ode in imitation of Horace (Ode *IX*, Lib. 1), which was published in the same year.

[12] Congreve to Moyle, 13 October 1695.

A Show'r of soft and fleecy Rain
Falls, to new-cloath the Earth again.
  Behold the Mountain-Tops, around,
  As if with Fur of Ermins crown'd:
  And lo! how by degrees
The universal Mantle hides the Trees,
  In hoary Flakes, which downward fly,
As if it were the *Autumn* of the Sky.

IV

Congreve had not been in the Middle Temple a year before the urge to publish came upon him. Digging out the manuscript of a short novel entitled *Incognita: or Love and Duty Reconcil'd*—which, according to some accounts, had been written four years earlier at Trinity College[13]—he sent it to press, shamefacedly leaving his name off, either because of the dubious reputation of novels at that period or else because the dignified law student did not care to acknowledge this trifle.

The sixty-page novelette is crowded with adventure arising from mistaken identity. Two young friends, Aurelian and Hippolito, withdrawing from school in Siena, come up to Florence just in time for the festivities of the great Duke, fall in love with two masques, break lances in the tournament, and after many dramatic episodes, win their ladies. Aurelian spends his time trying to avoid marrying Juliana, his father's choice for him, the jest being that Juliana and Aurelian's masqued sweetheart, Incognita, prove to be the same. Thus love and duty are easily reconciled.

Congreve attempted to give his story genuine Italian local color. His source of information was John Raymond's *An Itinerary contayning a Voyage made through Italy, in the years 1646 and 1647*, a copy of which has recently been found with Congreve's name on the title-page.[14] Some of the descriptive passages of the novel that give the truest Italian flavor are clearly drawn from Raymond's work. The plot, however, seems to be original. Perhaps Congreve derived the names of four of his characters, and something of the atmosphere and

---

[13] *Incognita* was licensed on December 22, 1691, and was published by Peter Buck about two months later. It was advertised in *The London Gazette*, No. 2742, for the period from February 18 to February 22, 1691/2. The novel had been written, according to Dr. Campbell's article in Biographia Britannica (1750), when the author was only seventeen.

[14] See E. S. deBeer, "Congreve's *Incognita:* The Source of its Setting, with a Note on Wilson's *Belphegor*," *RES*, VIII (1932), 74–77.

manner of the story, from Dryden's comedy, *The Assignation; or Love in a Nunnery*. But the plots of the novel and the play are entirely dissimilar.

If the average reader recalls that Congreve wrote poetry, he probably does not think of the poetic translations. And yet an examination of the poems in the collected editions will show that these translations occupy more than half of the total space. They were made, for the most part, during the years when Congreve was supposedly busy with the law. To his contemporaries this work was significant, and it gave him a certain dignity and prestige. To Congreve it was especially important because it was the means of beginning his warm friendship with the greatest poet of his age.

At this period Dryden had practically given over writing for the the stage and was turning for his livelihood to the translation of the Classics. About 1691 he planned a complete rendering of Juvenal. Five of the sixteen satires he translated himself, two he assigned to Nahum Tate, and the remaining nine he entrusted to as many individuals. The Juvenal was ready early in 1692, but Dryden held up publication in order that he might include his translation of the six satires of Persius. When the *Juvenal and Persius* was issued in October, 1692—with 1693 on the title page—it contained in the eleventh satire of Juvenal the first literary work to bear the name of William Congreve. To appear thus in the company of Dryden was a signal recognition for the young Middle Templar. Even more significant was the fact that Dryden published, by way of introduction to his own translation of *Persius*, Congreve's lines "To Mr. Dryden."

Earlier in the same year Congreve had given to his friend Charles Gildon two songs and three Pindaric odes for publication in a *Miscellany of Original Poems*. The following year he allowed the three odes to be reprinted under his name in Dryden's *Examen Poeticum*, and added translations of two passages from Homer. In the Dedication, Dryden called special attention to the contribution of "Mr. Congreve (whom I cannot mention without the honour which is due to his excellent parts, and that entire affection which I bear him)." "I wish," continued Dryden, "Mr. Congreve had the leisure to translate [the whole of Homer], and the world the good nature and justice to encourage him in that noble design, of which he is more capable than any man I know."

There is nothing mysterious in the friendship between Congreve and Dryden. Twenty-one and sixty, youth and age, were drawn together by common interests. The older poet found in the younger a literary taste and genius to command his respect, and affable man-

ners to win his affection. "I am Mr. Congreve's true lover," Dryden
wrote to Tonson, "and desire you to tell him, how kindly I take his
often remembrances of me: I wish him all prosperity, and hope I shall
never lose his affection." In 1692 we find Congreve going out to meet
Dryden on his return to London to keep him company "for the last
foure miles." He helped the old poet arrange with Tonson for the
translation of the Æneid.[15] And when Dryden and Tonson fell to
quarreling, Congreve, by virtue of his good sense and his firm friendship for both of them, was able to intervene effectively. "Mr. Congreve may be with us," writes Dryden to Tonson, "as a common
friend; for as you know him for yours, I make not the least doubt,
but he is much more mine."[16]

If Congreve the young Middle Templar made little progress in the
study of the law, as a literary man he did well. His pleasing manners
and sound learning won a large group of friends among the followers
of Dryden. And what is more remarkable, he secured their good will
without arousing their envy.

[15] The articles of agreement between Dryden and Tonson, witnessed by Congreve,
are preserved in the B. M. MS. Add. 36,933.

[16] For the quotations from Dryden's letters see *The Works of John Dryden*, ed.
Scott-Saintsbury (London, 1893), XVIII, 112, 122.

Chapter V

ENTER ANNE BRACEGIRDLE

I

WHILE Congreve was bringing out his novel and making poetic translations for Dryden, he had pushed to one side the manuscript of *The Old Bachelor*. When later he brought it, very hesitantly, to the attention of Dryden, the old dramatist at once pronounced it the best "first play" that he had ever seen. "The stuff," he said, "was rich indeed," and needed "only the fashionable cutt of the town."[1] Dryden himself went on to assist in the preparation of the play for the stage, cutting and rearranging the scenes. Gildon went so far as to say that Congreve's draft was "in nothing alter'd, but in the Length."[2]

No doubt the play submitted to Dryden had already undergone much polishing by the author. Congreve was, as Cibber said, "too judicious a Writer to let anything come hastily out of his Hands." In the nineteenth century there was a tradition that he had penned *The Old Bachelor* under a large oak near Stretton Hall; but a century earlier Dr. Johnson and Boswell, on a visit to Ilam in Dovedale, were shown a rocky ledge under which Congreve had written the same play. Perhaps both traditions are, in a measure, correct; for Congreve may have written his first draft at Stretton in 1689 and then revised it at Ilam, where he was certainly visiting in the autumn of 1692.

Congreve also had the assistance of Arthur Mainwaring, a fellow student of the law, and more particularly of Captain Thomas Southerne, to whom he had been introduced by his young military cousins. Southerne was ten years older than Congreve. Born in Dublin, he had preceded Congreve first at Trinity College and then at the Middle Temple. He had already produced four plays—two of them with marked success—and was in a position to befriend a young dramatist. He looked upon Congreve as his fellow countryman and was glad to join with Dryden in preparing Congreve's comedy for the stage. He recommended it to Thomas Davenant, then Manager of the Theatre Royal in Drury Lane, and secured for the young author the very unusual privilege of free admission to the playhouse a full six months prior to the acting of the play.

[1] Notes by Thomas Southerne, B. M Add. MSS. 4221, f. 341. Southerne also mentions the assistance given to Congreve by Arthur Mainwaring and himself.

[2] See Charles Gildon's ed. of Langbaine's *The Lives and Characters of the English Dramatick Poets* (London, 1699), p. 25.

Toward the close of 1692, after the play had been accepted and was perhaps already in rehearsal, the gifted actor William Mountfort was brutally murdered. Only a few weeks later two of the leading comedians died. The company was so disrupted that it was March, 1693, before *The Old Bachelor* was finally brought on the stage.[3] The unusual delay had served to advertize the play, and very probably the twelve hundred places in the Theatre Royal were filled before the first performance began at four o'clock on that March afternoon.[4]

The stage in this old Drury Lane Theatre was a strange affair. Somewhat in the manner of the Elizabethan stage, it jutted far out in front of the curtain and took a large semioval slice out of the pit. On this outer stage, the "apron," most of the acting took place. And as the players stood there, surrounded on three sides by their audience, they were almost a part of it. Even their entrances and exits were made chiefly through doors at either side of the apron just in front of the curtain and in full view of the spectators.

In the pit sat the young gentlemen from the Temple, the fops, and the beaux with their long perukes. Also in the pit near the stage assembled the critics, of caustic voice and calculating eye. Around them hovered the coffeehouse wits in velvet coats and flowing cravats. The orchestra of fiddles, lutes, and theorbos had rendered the

[3] January has usually been given as the month for the first performance of Congreve's comedy because *The Gentleman's Journal* for February announced the success of the play. But the "February" issue did not come out before the last of March or the first of April. In the "January" *Gentleman's Journal* which announced that *The Old Bachelor* would be "acted in a little time," the tardy editor was forced to admit, "We are now in *March*." The "February" issue was late enough to refer to the third printing of the play, which was announced in *The London Gazette* for March 23–27, 1693. See Albert S. Borgman, *The Life and Death of William Mountfort* (Cambridge: Harvard University Press, 1935), p 171. — It should also be noted that in the Epilogue Mrs. Barry implies that the lenten season (starting that year on February 28) had already begun.

[4] Early in the Restoration Period, on May 2, 1668, Pepys had gone to the theatre "at a little past twelve, to get a good place in the pit," had hired a man to keep his place, and had returned an hour later to "find the house quite full." The time for beginning the plays was then about three or three-thirty. By 1693 the time had been advanced to four o'clock; and by 1700 the regular time was five o'clock. An exterior view of Wren's Drury Lane Theatre, where Congreve's first play was acted, is reproduced by W. J. Lawrence, *The Elizabethan Playhouse and Other Studies*, Second Series (Stratford-upon-Avon, 1913), facing p. 106; a sectional design for the same theatre is reproduced, from the Library of All Souls College, Oxford, by Montague Summers, *The Restoration Theatre* (New York, 1934), facing p. 94. These two works, as well as Colley Cibber's *Apology*, ed. R. W. Lowe (London, 1889), Alwin Thaler's *Shakspere to Sheridan* (Cambridge: Harvard University Press, 1922), and Allardyce Nicoll's *A History of Restoration Drama, 1660–1700* (Cambridge University Press, 1923), give most helpful information about the Restoration stage.

"first" and the "second" music. As the "third" music, or "curtain tune" began, the audience became more conscious of the stage. The curtain tune came to an end. As the last note of fiddle, lute, and theorbo died away, Anne Bracegirdle stepped lightly out, wove her way through the beaux on the stage, and came well to the front of the apron, close up to the "floats," to speak the Prologue. Swinging out to the center of the stage on "her very handsome Legs and Feet,"[5] she veritably cast a spell upon the rowdy denizens of the pit. With her smiles, and her frowns, and her tears she held the swearing, gaming, frolicking pit in the palm of her hand. In the midst of her appeal for a favorable reception of the bashful young author, she pretended to forget her lines and ran off the stage in confusion. At some distance behind the place where she had stood, the curtains opened, revealing two gallants meeting in the street:

Bellmour. Vainlove, and abroad so early! good Morrow; I thought a Contemplative Lover could no more have parted with his Bed in a Morning, than a' could have slept in't.

Vainlove. Bellmour, good Morrow—Why truth on't is, these early Sallies are not usual to me; but Business, as you see Sir—(*Shewing Letters.*) And Business must be follow'd, or be lost.

Bell. Pox o' Business—And so must Time, my Friend, be close pursued, or lost. Business is the rub of Life, perverts our Aim, casts off the Bias, and leaves us wide and short of the intended Mark.

Vain. Pleasure, I guess you mean.

Bell. Ay, what else has meaning?

And so the tone of the dialogue was set—something more brilliant than Londoners were accustomed to. The audience expressed its approval of *The Old Bachelor* so enthusiastically that crowds continued to fill the house during fourteen days, a phonenal run for that period. In print the play was almost as popular as it had been on the stage. Before the end of the month it was in its third printing. *The Old Bachelor* became one of the most dependable plays in the repertoire of the theatre, to be acted many times each year. So particularly well liked were the Fondlewife scenes of the fourth act that they were frequently produced separately to supplement other theatrical enter-

---

[5] Descriptions of players given in Chapter V are taken from accounts left by two contemporary actors: (1) Cibber's *Apology*, ed. Lowe, I, 98 ff., especially 170 ff.; (2) Anthony Aston's *A Brief Supplement to Colley Cibber, Esq.; His Lives of the late Famous Actors and Actresses*, included by Lowe in his edition of Cibber's *Apology*, II, 297–318.

ANNE BRACEGIRDLE

tainments. Of all Congreve's comedies, only *Love for Love* has had a more lasting popularity.

The initial triumph of *The Old Bachelor* owed much to the unusual theatrical talent then available. The union of the two companies ten years before had brought together at the Theatre Royal in Drury Lane the best actors that England could afford. At the head of the united company was Thomas Betterton, still in his prime after forty-two years on the stage, with seventeen years more of effective acting before his career would be over. With his sturdy figure, his "short thick Neck," and his "low and grumbling" voice, he was perfectly cast for Heartwell, the surly Old Bachelor.

Among the women of the company, Elizabeth Barry occupied a place almost as distinguished as that of Betterton among the men. Trained and brought on the stage by the Earl of Rochester about twenty years before, she was soon recognized as the most gifted of Restoration actresses. Anne Bracegirdle, great actress though she was and certainly the darling of the playhouse in 1693, graciously acknowledged the supreme talent of the older woman. In *The Old Bachelor* Mrs. Barry took the important part of Laetitia, young wife of the old banker, Fondlewife.

The comic part, Fondlewife, was the crucial rôle of the play. The great comedian Anthony Leigh, whom Charles II delighted in calling "his actor," had died only a few months before. As old Fondlewife he would have been sure to delight the audience. But perhaps Congreve was happy to see the part in the hands of his good friend Thomas Doggett, who had come over from the Smock Alley Theatre the same year that Congreve came up to London. While the one was keeping terms at the Middle Temple, the other was rapidly gaining recognition in comic rôles at Drury Lane. Doggett fully justified the confidence placed in him. To his acting, in the opinion of Cibber, *The Old Bachelor* "probably ow'd the greatest Part of its Success."

But of all the parts in *The Old Bachelor* Congreve followed most intently that of Araminta. For with Anne Bracegirdle, the creator of that capricious heroine, he had fallen madly in love. Anne, still in her twenties, was seven years older than Congreve. She was the daughter of Richard Bracegirdle, of Wolverhampton, by his second wife Dorothea Chetwynd, of Ridsley.[6] Since Anne's father had been married

---

[6] Even during her lifetime Anne Bracegirdle was thought to be the daughter of Justinian Bracegirdle, of Northampton. Anthony Aston (*A Brief Supplement*, in Cibber's *Apology*, ed. Lowe, II, 303) mentioned the general opinion but asserted his own belief that she was from Wolverhampton or Walsal, Staffordshire. Dugdale's Visitation shows that Aston was correct.

three times and had eleven children, he welcomed the opportunity to have her brought up in the family of the famous actor Thomas Betterton. She is said to have acted the part of the page in Otway's *The Orphan* at the age of six—evidently an error for sixteen, since Otway's play was not brought on the stage till 1680. Before 1690 Anne Bracegirdle was appearing regularly in plays at Drury Lane and was then, according to Cibber, "just blooming to her Maturity: her Reputation as an Actress gradually rising with that of her Person." Cibber goes on to say that "never any Woman was in such general Favour of her Spectators . . . Scarce an Audience saw her that were less than half of them Lovers." She was "the Universal Passion . . . She inspired the best Authors to write for her, and two of them [Congreve and Rowe], when they gave her a Lover in a Play, seem'd palpably to plead their own Passions, and make their private Court to her in fictitious Characters."

Her reputation for strict chastity—a rare grace among the actresses of that day—had gone far toward making her the darling of the whole audience. The actor Anthony Aston tells how, on one occasion, Lord Halifax, Dorset, and others gathered around a bottle of wine to commend "this incomparable Woman," and ended by sending her eight hundred pounds "with Encomiums on her Virtue." Aston gives us a charming picture of Anne:

She was of a lovely Height, with dark-brown Hair and Eye-brows, black sparkling Eyes, and a fresh blushy Complexion; and, whenever she exerted herself, had an involuntary Flushing in her Breast, Neck and Face, having continually a chearful Aspect, and a fine Set of even white Teeth; never making an *Exit*, but that she left the Audience in an Imitation of her pleasant Countenance.

It was no wonder, then, that young Will Congreve came under the spell of Anne Bracegirdle. Not only was he a spectator when she acted at Drury Lane; he was also a member of that smaller, more intimate group at the rehearsals of *The Old Bachelor*. And those rehearsals, we must remember, were extended by untimely deaths among the actors to nearly half a year. Before the play was finally ready for its first triumphant performance, Congreve had probably penned the well-known lines in which he was forced to admit that he had not yet triumphed in his efforts to win his "Pious Selinda,"[7] that "Diana of the stage," as his mistress.

> Pious *Selinda* goes to Pray'rs,
> If I but ask the Favour;

[7] Aston says specifically (II, 304) that Mrs. Bracegirdle is the person referred to by "Pious Selinda." The poem is printed from the edition by Dobrée, p. 245.

And yet the tender Fool's in Tears,
When she believes I'll leave her.

Wou'd I were free from this Restraint,
Or else had hopes to win her;
Wou'd she cou'd make of me a Saint,
Or I of her a Sinner.

Congreve was desperately in love with Anne. He was much less interested in becoming a "Saint" than in inducing her to become a "Sinner." And Anne was not a cold, unfeeling beauty. She was only too "tender" toward the young dramatist who showed "his assiduity by following" her and who was "the most entertaining sort of animal imaginable."[8] Why then did not Congreve marry Anne Bracegirdle? Who knows? One may guess that it was not the way of the world, of Congreve's world—or, for that matter, of Anne Bracegirdle's. We do know that Congreve did not let the restraint of his Pious Selinda deter him in his pursuit of her. Hardly had *The Old Bachelor* ended its first run before he was writing for Anne Bracegirdle the part of the virtuous heroine Cynthia of *The Double-Dealer*.[9] In the rôle of the lover Mellefont, as Cibber rightly observed, Congreve was pleading his own passion.

II

During the summer of 1693 Congreve went out of London to a quiet place beyond Lenoch. The winsome youth of Kilkenny days, now twenty-three, had matured fast. But the droop of his shoulders still suggested a lack of ruggedness. The long, flowing curls (now a wig) still framed a sensitive oval face. The nose had become more aquiline. The childish twinkle had given way to a steady, questioning look. The chin had lost its firmness, and the puffed lips suggested complacency with life which had treated him well thus far. The bright blue waistcoat and neatly swirled cravat brought back vividly the memory of a carefully groomed lad in Kilkenny who bore the stamp of gentle birth and breeding.[10]

The natural restraint which had been his in his boyhood, and his sensitiveness to beauty and quiet, had increased with the years and were dominant in the man who now wished to escape the hero worship

[8] Tom Brown, *Amusements Serious and Comical and Other Works*, ed. Arthur L. Hayward (London, 1927), p. 32.

[9] *The Gentleman's Journal* for February 1692/3—actually appearing about April—mentioned (p. 61) Congreve's preparation of another play to follow *The Old Bachelor*.

[10] Cf. the portraits of Congreve by Henry Tilson (frontispiece) and by Clarea (opposite page 18)

that inevitably comes to a successful author. The haven to which he was slipping away he spoke of as a "pretty retirement." "I shall leave this place with great regrett," he wrote Tonson, "having never in my life been better pleased for the time." He found there, along with the peace, "good air, moderate exercise, temperate living perfect ease & plenty."[11] And yet, in spite of all this, his health was not good. He complained of vapours and of heat in the palms of his hands, so that he felt himself obliged, much against his will, to go over to Epsom for the waters. But the "noisy pleasures" there repelled him, as did the thought of the London crowds on his way through the city to Epsom. So he asked Tonson to say nothing of his stop in London: he wanted to come and go quietly.

After his return to London in the autumn, Congreve soon had his new comedy ready for Drury Lane, where it was produced about the beginning of December, 1693. On December 12 Dryden wrote to William Walsh: "His Double Dealer is much censured by the greater part of the Town: and is defended only by the best judges, who, you know, are commonly the fewest yet it gets ground daily, and has already been acted Eight times." Another contemporary wrote: "It has fared with that play, as it generally does with beauties officiously cried up; the mighty expectation which was raised of it made it sink even beneath its own merit."[12]

The Double-Dealer had the least applause of any of Congreve's plays. In fact it came very close to being hissed off the stage. Congreve was doubly sensitive to the harsh criticism after the kindly reception of The Old Bachelor, a play which he knew was inferior. He was a good enough critic of his own work to recognize the serious defects of his first comedy. He worked conscientiously to give his audience a more solid play, believed that he had done so, and consequently was perplexed and irritated by the result.

In the Dedication Congreve sadly lost his wonted amiability and evenness of temper. "I hear," he wrote, "a great many of the Fools are angry at me, and I am glad of it; for I Writ at them, not to 'em." His "Illiterate Criticks," "snarling and barking" their "Impotent Objections," were swayed, he insisted, by "Ignorance and Malice." Later, as his anger cooled, he thought better of his critics and removed this hastily written invective from the next edition of the play.

[11] Congreve to Tonson, Tuesday [1693]; Congreve to a Lady, 9 August [1693].
[12] See J. O. Halliwell, A Dictionary of Old English Plays (London, 1860), pp. 77, 78. The Gentleman's Journal for "November" (actually issued in December, 1693, or later) mentions (p. 374) the recent production of The Double-Dealer. Publication of the play was announced by the London Gazette for 4–7 December 1693.

Dryden had written Walsh that the women were displeased with *The Double-Dealer* because it "exposed their Bitchery too much." This charge Congreve answered by saying:

It is the Business of a Comick Poet to paint the Vices and Follies of Human-kind. . . . I should be very glad of an Opportunity to make my Compliment to those Ladies who are offended: But they can no more expect it in a Comedy, than to be Tickled by a Surgeon, when he's letting 'em Blood. They who are Virtuous or Discreet, should not be offended, for such Charac-ters as these distinguish *them*, and make their Beauties more shining and observ'd: And they who are of the other kind, may nevertheless pass for such, by seeming not to be displeas'd, or touch'd with the Satire of this *Comedy*.

What Congreve lost in popular applause was made up by a chorus of the "best judges," with Dryden at their head. The old poet wrote seventy-seven eloquent lines "To My Dear Friend Mr. Congreve, on his Comedy call'd *The Double-Dealer*," closing with this passage:

> Maintain your Post: That's all the Fame you need;
> For 'tis impossible you shou'd proceed.
> Already I am worn with Cares and Age;
> And just abandoning th' Ungrateful Stage:
> Unprofitably kept at Heav'ns Expence,
> I live a Rent-charge on his Providence:
> But You, whom ev'ry Muse and Grace adorn,
> Whom I forsee to better Fortune born,
> Be kind to my Remains; and oh defend,
> Against your Judgment, your departed Friend!
> Let not th' insulting Foe my Fame pursue;
> But shade those Lawrels which descend to You:
> And take for Tribute what these Lines express:
> You merit more; nor cou'd my Love do less.

Addison, in his *Account of the Greatest English Poets*, seconded Dry-den's praise:

> How might we fear our English poetry,
> That long has flourished, should decay with thee [Dryden];
> Did not the muses' other hope appear,
> Harmonious Congreve, and forbid our fear:
> Congreve! whose fancy's unexhausted store
> Has given already much, and promised more.
> Congreve shall still preserve thy fame alive,
> And Dryden's muse shall in his friend survive.

A tribute perhaps less eloquent, but certainly no less sincere, came from the pen of Congreve's old schoolfellow and college friend,

Jonathan Swift. Three years older than Congreve, Swift had taken
his bachelor's degree the year Congreve came up from Kilkenny, but
he stayed on in residence at Trinity College until the Revolution and
then, like Congreve, withdrew to England. They may have crossed
the Irish Sea together. While Congreve stopped with his grandfather
at Stretton, Swift probably went on to join his mother in neighboring
Leicestershire.

It is interesting to observe how differently the two friends impressed Dryden. Congreve was a man about town and a literary
Middle Templar. His scholarship, his translations, and his affability
endeared him to Dryden. Swift in the meantime was at Moor Park
tutoring "Stella" and composing poetry. There in the home of Temple
he wrote a Pindaric ode to his patron, another to King William, and
a third to the Athenian Society. Armed with these, he sought out
Dryden, to whom he was probably introduced by Congreve at Will's.
The old poet's hard verdict, "Cousin Swift, you will never be a poet,"
earned Swift's eternal hatred.

But for Congreve Swift continued to have only love and esteem.
Before *The Double-Dealer* was in the press, he had prepared 234 lines
"to Mr. Congreve." Confused and difficult as the poem often is, it
rings with friendship:

> Godlike the force of my young Congreve's bays,
> Softening the Muse's thunder into praise . . .
> Gets between them [critics] and my resentment's weight,
> Stands in the gap 'twixt me and wretched men,
> T' avert th' impending judgments of my pen.
>   Thus I look down with mercy on the age,
> By hopes my Congreve will reform the stage:
> For never did poetic mind before
> Produce a richer vein, or clearer ore.

The generous support of friends had softened the sting of dis-
gruntled critics. Then, about a month after the somewhat uncertain
first run of *The Double-Dealer*, Queen Mary ordered a special performance. Cibber tells of this event with enthusiasm because the sickness of one of the regular actors gave him a chance to act the part of
Lord Touchwood. Congreve got the part for Cibber and was so delighted with his acting that he had his weekly salary increased from
fifteen to twenty shillings. Cibber quotes from memory two lines
from a prologue which he says was written specially for the occasion.
But he was mistaken. The lines occur in a prologue which, according
to Congreve, was written for a special performance of *The Old Bachelor* ordered later by the Queen. When Queen Mary died of smallpox

the following year, Congreve gratefully wrote in her memory *The Mourning Muse of Alexis*. This pastoral pleased the age, and King William—who seldom gave largess to the poets—ordered that one hundred pounds be given to the author.[13]

III

In the meantime Congreve was not forgetting Anne Bracegirdle. He took great delight in watching her on the stage. "She looks to a miracle," said Tom Brown, "when she is acting a part in one of his own plays."[14] Congreve made it his practice to sit in one of the little side boxes very near the stage, with hat pulled down well over his eyes[15]— for his eyes were troubling him even then—lost to all the world save one. Outside the theatre he saw much of Anne, rode with her, and visited her "in public and private." He is reported to have dined with her "almost every day."[16] It was even rumored that he had secretly married her.

But what was actually the relationship between Congreve and Mrs. Bracegirdle? What were contemporaries saying? Of the voluminous gossip that must have passed current through all London, the opinions of Antony Aston, Tom Brown, Colley Cibber, Charles Gildon, and Jonathan Swift have come down to us. Aston was outspoken in his championship of Mrs. Bracegirdle: "She had many Assailants on her Virtue, as Lord *Lovelace*, Mr. *Congreve*, the last of which had her Company most; but she ever resisted his vicious Attacks, and, yet, was always uneasy at his leaving her."[17] The notorious Tom Brown was no less positive in his repeated assertion of an opposite opinion. But Brown and Aston, closely associated with neither Congreve nor Mrs. Bracegirdle, spoke with little authority. With Cibber the case was different. Though he was never intimate with Congreve, he was closely associated with Mrs. Bracegirdle until she withdrew from the Theatre Royal in 1695. Throughout the remainder of her long life he was on most friendly terms with her. And we must remember that she was still living when Cibber published his

---

[13] See Narcissus Luttrell, *A Brief Historical Relation of State Affairs* (Oxford, 1857), III, 435.

[14] *Amusements Serious and Comical and Other Works*, ed. Arthur L. Hayward, pp. 32, 33.

[15] See The Preface to *Animadversions on Mr. Congreve's Late Answer to Mr. Collier* (London, 1698).

[16] Tom Brown, *op. cit.*

[17] See Cibber's *Apology*, ed. Lowe, II, 304. For Tom Brown's opinion see *Amusements Serious and Comical and Other Works*, ed. Arthur L. Hayward, pp. 32, 33, 378, 435–438.

Apology. He was keenly aware that Mrs. Bracegirdle would read what he said of her, and he admitted that he was recalling her youth in "the most favourable Light." He did emphasize her great reputation for chastity, her "Discretion," and her "not being unguarded in her private Character."[18] But some of Cibber's phrases remain open to two interpretations.

The opinions most worthy of consideration are those of Charles Gildon and Jonathan Swift, men who were really intimate with Congreve. Gildon expressed himself incidentally in 1702, in a dialogue entitled *A Comparison between the Two Stages:*

Sullen. But does that Romantick Virgin [Bracegirdle] still keep up her great Reputation?

Critick. D'ye mean her Reputation for Acting?

Sullen. I mean her Reputation for not Acting; you understand me—

Critick. I do; but if I were to be sav'd for believeing that single Article, I cou'd not do't: 'Tis all, all a Juggle, 'tis Legerdemain; the best on't is, she falls into good Hands, and the secrecy of the Intrigue secures her; but as to her Innocence, I believe no more on't than I believe of *John Mandevil.*

Gildon's "secrecy of the Intrigue" is not greatly different from one possible interpretation of Cibber's "Discretion" and "not being unguarded."

Swift's opinion of Mrs. Bracegirdle carries even more weight because it was expressed in a personal letter to Charles Ford. Not written till 1724, it gives Swift's reasoned judgment. "I sometimes think," wrote Swift, "D. Wharton intends to take my Advice of fancying to have Virtue. I remember Mrs. Bracegirdle got more by acting that Part than any of the more abandoned Playhouse females, there is a sort of a Contrast in it."[19]

Possibly, then, Anne Bracegirdle was not always the unrelenting Selinda. Indeed, it may be that happiness in a mutual love played its part in the years just ahead, when Congreve went on to write his most successful plays, and Mrs. Bracegirdle to do the supreme acting of her career. Congreve did not overlook her phenomenal success in making that special appeal to the favor of the audience with which Restoration plays opened and closed. For each of his plays she appeared either in the Prologue or in the Epilogue. Well might the audience be won to sympathetic attention by Anne's grace and

---

[18] Cibber's *Apology*, ed. Lowe, I, 170.
[19] *The Letters of Jonathan Swift to Charles Ford*, ed. David Nichol Smith (Oxford, 1935), p. 107.

charm.[20] Well might it—even if undecided at the close of the play whether to praise or to damn—be led by the winsome actress to applaud. For, as Congreve made her say in the Epilogue to *Love for Love*, she had a "begging Face" too appealing for an audience to deny.

Love for Love was ready for the stage late in 1694, and would have been presented at Drury Lane except for the renewal of the old controversy between the patentees and the players. Congreve very judiciously withheld his play, thus reserving it for the new company that was to begin acting the following year in Lincoln's Inn Fields.[21]

This new company, headed by Betterton and composed of practically all the players who had acted in Congreve's first two comedies, had been forced into revolt by the unreasonable attitude of those in control at Drury Lane. Since the Restoration, the producing of plays in London had been the exclusive right of two companies, the King's and the Duke's. So long as these companies were rivals, players abused by the one could turn to the other. But after the two joined forces in 1682, the players were entirely at the mercy of the united patentees, who felt themselves secure in a monopoly that nothing could disturb. The patentees neglected the players, ignored their just complaints, and created among them a general unrest. The audience took the side of the players and appealed to the Earl of Dorset, who was then Lord Chamberlain. He secured the legal opinion that "no Patent for acting Plays, &c. could tie up the Hands of a succeeding Prince." In other words, the monopoly granted by Charles II on which the patentees had relied so confidently could be broken. On March 25, 1695, King William issued a separate license to Betterton, Mrs. Barry, Mrs. Bracegirdle, Bowman, Williams, Underhill, Doggett, Bowen, Mrs. Verbruggen, Mrs. Leigh, and Bright.[22]

Congreve naturally cast his lot with Mrs. Bracegirdle. He took such an active part in the formation of the new company that John Downes, the old prompter at Drury Lane, later mentioned him as one of the original sharers. But Congreve is not mentioned in the warrant issued by the Lord Chamberlain, and for this reason it seems

[20] See Autrey Nell Wiley, "Female Prologues and Epilogues in English Plays," *PMLA*, XLVIII (1933), 1067.

[21] The chief sources for theatrical conditions in London at the end of the seventeenth century are Cibber's *Apology*, Aston's *Supplement*, John Downes' *Roscius Anglicanus*, and Gildon's ed. of Langbaine. Cibber joined the company acting at the Drury Lane Theatre in 1690. He tells of the reasons underlying the revolt led by Betterton (I, 181 ff.), of the competition between the two theatres (I, 194 ff.), and of Congreve's narrow escape from having *Love for Love* acted at Drury Lane (I, 197).

[22] P. R. O., Lord Chamberlain Papers 7/1, 7/3. The license is printed by Nicoll *Restoration Drama*, p. 323.

probable, as Cibber implies, that Congreve did not receive a share in the company until after the successful production of his *Love for Love*.

For a playhouse Betterton turned to the old Lisle Tennis Court in Lincoln's Inn Fields, which had, on several occasions, been used temporarily as a theatre. The remodeling necessary was made easy by the enthusuastic support of wealthy patrons, who contributed from twenty to forty pounds each. On Tuesday, April 30, 1695, the new theatre was ready for the first play—Congreve's *Love for Love*.

Any play would have been received with applause, for the audience was determined to encourage the revolting players. The author of The *Comparison between the Two Stages* (1702) said of *Love for Love* that "the Town was ingag'd in its favour, and in favour of the Actors long before the Play was Acted." The comedy answered all expectations and continued before full houses for thirteen successive days. Doggett was a glorious Sailor Ben. Ned Ward tells us how the belated beaux do "squeeze into the *Pit*, when . . . Dogget in *Love for Love*, is to play Son Benjamin." Cibber tells us that "they had seldom occasion to act any other Play 'till the End of the Season." The popular success of *Love for Love* was entirely deserved: if not the best among Congreve's comedies, at least it is the most actable. The company offered Congreve a full share with them, and he accepted it, with the promise to write exclusively for Betterton's group and to provide one new play yearly.

About two weeks after the first performance, *Love for Love* was published with a dedication to Charles Sackville, Earl of Dorset. Descended from the Elizabethan poet of the *Mirror for Magistrates*, Dorset added further literary distinction to his family name by writing the famous ballad, "To all you ladies now at land." He had a genuine interest in the theatre and was glad, as Lord Chamberlain, to encourage the Betterton group. He, more than anyone else, was responsible for the success of the revolting players. It was a very fitting tribute on the part of Congreve to dedicate to him the first play acted by the new company. Dorset placed Congreve's portrait on the walls of his Poet's Parlor at Knole. When the old Earl lay at Knole on his deathbed ten years later, Congreve visited him and came away remarking, "Faith, he slabbers more wit dying than other people do in their best health."[23]

[23] See V. Sackville-West, *Knole and the Sackvilles* (London, 1922), p. 141.

IV

Soon after the production of *Love for Love* Congreve received his first political appointment. At that period government sinecures were very commonly given to literary men to secure them to the interest of the ruling party. The Whigs, in their efforts to ensure the success of the Revolution by popularizing King William and the war with Louis XIV, could well afford to subsidize an eloquent pen. Congreve was a loyal party man, a Whig strong for the principles of the Revolution, with a literary fame that gave him a wide hearing. His lament on the death of Queen Mary was in a measure a party poem. More specifically political were his Pindaric lines "To the King, on the Taking of Namure," 1695, and later odes in praise of King William, Marlborough, Sidney Godolphin, and other Whig leaders.

The extent to which Congreve was rewarded by his party has been greatly exaggerated. The usual notion of Congreve's easy life as a government official is that given currency by Thackeray. He evidently believed that, soon after the staging of *The Old Bachelor*, Congreve's political friends threw into his lap a plurality of sinecures sufficient to make the rest of his days carefree. He pictured Congreve "in a state of ease and tranquillity," with a "commissionership of hackney-coaches—a post in the Custom-house—a place in the Pipe-office, and all for writing a comedy!"[24]

Swift knew better. He was in the thick of the political strife of his day, and he was following with full sympathy the career of his old schoolfellow. Through many an evening in London he sat with Congreve over a bottle of wine. Swift was not writing from mere hearsay when he recorded many years later that Congreve had spent in "one poor office, half his days."[25] But we have ignored Congreve's contemporary and have listened to the Victorian. Fortunately we need have no question whether Swift or Thackeray was correct. The original documents showing the extent and nature of Congreve's government service are still preserved at the Public Record Office in London.

Congreve held no lucrative political office till the last years of his life. Even his first minor appointment did not follow immediately the production of *The Old Bachelor*, nor that of *The Double-Dealer*. Not until the summer of 1695, after *Love for Love* had brought Congreve almost to the height of his reputation, did he become one of the five Commissioners for Licensing Hackney Coaches. The post then be-

[24] *English Humourists of the Eighteenth Century* (London, 1853) pp. 58, 59.

[25] See "A Libel on the Reverend Dr. Delany, and His Excellency John, Lord Carteret," *The Poems of Jonathan Swift, D. D.*, ed. W. E. Browning (London, 1910), I, 321.

came his because the annual salary was reduced by half, and three of the old commissioners refused to serve longer.[26] The office for the commissioners was in Surrey Street, between the Strand and the river, only a stone's throw west of Congreve's residence in Arundel Street. The real work was done by a secretary, a housekeeper, two messengers, and two streetkeepers. To the commissioners fell the general supervision and occasional reports to the Lords of the Treasury.

This post took up little time. It left Congreve plenty of leisure to write the one play yearly that he had promised his company, "if his health permitted." Although this phrase is a commonplace in such agreements, it had special significance in the case of Congreve. The love for good food and good wine, which he had indulged from his school days, was beginning to have its effect. Swift tells us that it was Congreve's "misfortune to squander away a very good constitution in his younger days," a loss which Swift regrets the more because "a man of sense and merit like him, is bound in conscience to preserve his health for the sake of his friends, as well as of himself."[27] As early as the summer of 1693 Congreve had been forced to resort to Tunbridge Wells, and then to transfer to Epsom in the hope of getting more relief from the waters there. The next summer he was at Windsor lamenting that he was too sick to meet the beautiful singer, Arabella Hunt, at Epsom. During the summer following the successful run of *Love for Love*, Congreve went again to Tunbridge, and this time with better results. He wrote to John Dennis that he had found there a "good Stomach," which was to him a "new Acquaintance." The pleasant tone of the letter is that of the dyspeptic relieved for once of a gnawing pain and revelling in a good appetite, which he compares to that of an ostrich.

The summer of 1695 was perhaps the happiest of his life. Once more, for a short period, he had the good health and good appetite of

---

[26] Under date of 6 June 1695, *The Post Boy* has the following entry: "The Sallery of the Commissioners for Licensing of Hackney and Stage-coaches being reduced to 100 l. *per Annum*, Mr. *Ashurst*, Mr. *Overbury* and Mr. *Isham* resigned their places, and are to be succeeded by Mr. *Herne*, Mr. *Clark* and Mr. *Congreve*." Congreve's patent was dated 12 July 1695. See P. R. O., Patent Roll 3378, 7 William III, Part I, No. 1. Although Congreve was not appointed until the summer, 1695, he was paid quarterly from 25 March 1695 till the end of his term at Christmas, 1705. See the Declared Accounts of the Commissioners at the Public Record Office for the years ending from midsummer, 1696, to midsummer, 1706.

[27] See Swift's letter to Pope on 13 February 1728/9. Congreve's movements to promote his health during the summers of 1693, 1694, and 1695 can be traced by means of his letters to Tonson (LIX, LX), Arabella Hunt (LVII), and Dennis (XLV).

his boyhood, and he could now enjoy them more, for he had known what it was to be without these blessings. The success of his last comedy had removed the doubts raised eighteen months before by *The Double-Dealer* and had thoroughly justified the confidence then expressed by his close friends. It had also provided funds for his immediate needs and had given him faith in his ability to make his way by his pen. His important critical essay *Concerning Humour in Comedy*, written at the first of the summer, showed a growing faith in himself. His financial independence seemed further assured by the full share now given to him in the thriving new theatrical company. And finally, his post as Licenser for Hackney Coaches seemed to the young dramatist, in the summer of 1695, only the first step on the easy way to fat government employments. A few years later he was to learn that political office was no more to be relied on than the favor of the audience for his own artistic efforts or the continued popularity of the company in which he was a sharer. But in the summer of 1695 he did not know all this. He seemed to have dependable sources of income, his good health had returned, and Anne Bracegirdle was both charming and kind. There was reason for the buoyant tone of his letters.

V

While Congreve was still at Tunbridge, his publisher Jacob Tonson —who was also his close friend—wrote to offer his assistance in the entertainment of Congreve's mother. Possibly Mrs. Congreve had come over from Ireland earlier in the year for the production of her son's new comedy and was visiting her relations in the country while Congreve was at Tunbridge. At any rate, on his return from Tunbridge Congreve was expecting his mother to come up to London for a period.[28] The dramatist's parents were then living at Lismore Castle, Ireland, beautiful and stately old seat of the Earl of Cork and Burlington, where the father was supervising the Earl's Irish estates. With this new work, Congreve's father dropped permanently out of the army, but not before he had been promoted to the rank of colonel. This title appeared before his name in the Lismore account books as early as 1691, and was used regularly throughout the remaining twelve years of his residence at Lismore.

Colonel Congreve's position with the Burlington estate is made clear by his account books still preserved at the Castle. The post was one of dignity and responsibility. As resident agent at Lismore Castle he was chief representative of the Earl of Burlington in Ireland. His

[28] See Congreve's letter to Tonson (LXI).

yearly salary of one hundred pounds was high for that period, as is shown by the fact that no other employee received more than fifty pounds. Even Colonel Digby Fowke, agent at Youghal, received only fifty pounds until Colonel Congreve withdrew from the service at the end of 1702, when, as chief agent, he was advanced to eighty pounds. Besides his regular salary, Colonel Congreve was allowed "Rideing Charges" of twenty pounds yearly, a personal servant whose wages were taken care of by the estate, and other perquisites. Further, he was provided with very pleasant and spacious lodgings for himself and for the members of his family in the east wing of the Castle overlooking the gardens. There it fell to the lot of Colonel and Mrs. Congreve, as representatives of the Earl and Countess—who were then regular residents on their English estates—to entertain judges and other dignitaries visiting Lismore. In March, 1698, the Colonel was paid three pounds and thirteen shillings "for entertaining the Judges at Lismore Castle," and on another occasion Mrs. Congreve presented a special entertainment bill amounting to more than five pounds, including ten pence "she'd laid out for Candles."

The prominence of the Colonel's position led to various appointments. In 1695 he was named one of the Commissioners of Supply for the county of Waterford and was reappointed in 1697 and in 1698.[29] A year later he was made Deputy Governor for the County under the Earl of Tyrone.[30] Colonel Congreve continued to make his home at Lismore Castle until the fall of 1702. Soon after passing his sixty-fifth birthday, in September of that year, he collected his last quarterly salary, was placed on a pension at half pay, and returned to England to spend his last years.

The twelve years spent by Colonel and Mrs. Congreve at Lismore Castle cover the full period of their son's active literary career. It would be interesting to know how many times during that period the young dramatist was a guest with his parents in the east end of the Castle overlooking the gardens. In the correspondence with Keally, which does not begin till 1697, Congreve twice mentions proposed visits to Ireland, and he writes of them in such a casual way as to indicate that these visits were not out of the ordinary.

It seems probable that Congreve spent a part of 1696 in Ireland. During the previous year he had been unusually busy with the organization of the new dramatic company and the production of *Love for Love*. His whereabouts can be traced during the summer of 1695

[29] See *The Statutes at Large, Passed in the Parliaments held in Ireland*, III, 1665–1698 (Dublin, 1765).

[30] See *Journal of the Royal Society of Antiquaries of Ireland*, 6th Ser., XV (1925), 39.

LISMORE CASTLE (two views)
Residence of Congreve's father and mother from
1691 to 1702

by his correspondence with Dennis, and during the autumn by his correspondence with Walter Moyle. Toward the end of the year Congreve was assisting Dryden with the production of his son's comedy, for which Congreve wrote the Epilogue. Then follows a year, 1696, during which Congreve's record in England is a blank. The season of 1695–1696 came and went without any play from Congreve; and it was near the end of the following season, in the spring of 1697, before he brought his next play on the stage. During this interval in which we find no mention of Congreve in England, a significant entry appears in the Irish records, in the Minutes of the Provost and Fellows of Trinity College, Dublin, for 19 February 1695/6: "The same day Mr. Tho. Southern and Mr. Will Congreve had the grace of ye house for ye Degree of Master of Arts." Evidently Congreve and Southern had crossed over to Dublin to be honored by the Irish university.

Once in Ireland, Congreve probably went on down to spend the summer with his father and mother at Lismore. From the quiet of the old castle he could look out on a well-kept garden sloping gently to a clump of ancient yew trees; or from another side, he could look down steep banks to the swift current of the Blackwater, the Irish Rhine. Lismore was a pleasant retreat from the street cries of London and the chatter of the beaux at Will's or the Grecian. No one could hold with more ease than Congreve a place among the wits of the London coffeehouses; and yet he was glad to get away from that life. He did not, so he wrote Keally, always "choose . . . to conform" himself "to the manners of . . . court or chocolate-house acquaintance." Secluded Lismore, with his parents, must therefore have had a very definite appeal.

The site of Lismore Castle was picturesque, and the dignity and age of that old fortress were in keeping with the mood of the tragedy Congreve was then polishing. One of the oldest castles in an old country, it had witnessed scenes no less stirring than those Congreve was depicting in *The Mourning Bride*. Hundreds of years before he wrote his heroic play, the monks of the neighboring Cathedral of St. Carthagh had been led by the tragic events in Ireland to hide deep in the bowels of the old baronial castle a whole library of the deeds of Celtic heroes—the famous *Book of Lismore*. Perhaps Congreve drew from Lismore Castle and the old cathedral nearby the inspiration for that passage which Dr. Johnson thought unsurpassed in "the whole mass of English poetry":

Almeria.
It was a fancy'd Noise, for all is hush'd.

Leonora.

It bore the Accent of a Human Voice.

Almeria.

It was thy Fear, or else some transient Wind
Whistling thro' Hollows of this vaulted Isle.
We'll listen—

Leonora.

Hark!

Almeria.

No, all is hush'd, and still as Death—
  'Tis dreadful!
How reverend is the Face of this tall Pile,
Whose ancient Pillars rear their Marble Heads,
To bear aloft its arch'd and pond'rous Roof,
By its own Weight made steadfast and immoveable,
Looking Tranquility. It striks an Awe
And Terror on my aking Sight; the Tombs
And Monumental Caves of Death look cold,
And shoot a Chilness to my trembling Heart.
Give me thy Hand, and let me hear thy Voice;
Nay, quickly speak to me, and let me hear
Thy Voice—my own affrights me with its Echo's.

Before the production of *The Mourning Bride* it was difficult for
the playgoers of the period to think of Congreve as a writer of tragedy.
His first three plays, comedies of manners, were definitely in the
tradition of Etherege and Wycherley, playwrights who had been content to limit themselves to witty attacks on the vices of the age. But
Congreve's interest in heroic romance need not surprise anyone who
has read his early novel *Incognita*. Soon after Congreve had published
the novel, and while he was writing and producing *The Double-Dealer*
and *Love for Love*, he was planning his tragedy. In 1693 Swift wrote
that Congreve intended "to write heroics next," and mentioned the
current view that tragedy would not fit his genius—in fact, would
"lose" him "quite." Two years later Walter Moyle was inquiring of
Congreve what progress he was making with his tragedy. Not until
the spring of 1697 was the play sufficiently polished to be entrusted
to the actors; and even after it had been produced and published, the
author continued to revise it for later editions.

The play was brought on the stage at Lincoln's Inn Fields on Saturday, 27 February 1697, and, according to Downes, "continu'd
Acting Uninterrupted 13 Days together." A London gentleman writing three days after the end of the first run is authority that the

theatre "was full to the last."[31] Congreve had surprised his public
by his ability to write effectively in a serious vein. A contemporary
noted that the play "far exceeded what the world expected from him
in that part of dramatic poetry."[32] When Sir Richard Blackmore
published his *King Arthur* a few months later, he made in his Preface
an extended eulogy of *The Mourning Bride.* "This *Poem,*" he wrote,
"has receiv'd, and in my Opinion very justly, Universal Applause;
being look'd on as the most perfect *Tragedy* that has been wrote in
this Age."

The Mourning Bride was Congreve's most popular play. Charles
Gildon even called it the "greatest Success . . . that ever I can remember on the English Stage." It was naturally the most profitable
for the author; for Congreve now had, in addition to his regular benefit nights, a full share in the profits of the company. The play continued popular during Congreve's period and throughout the whole
of the eighteenth century. Although it dropped out of the theatrical
repertoire over a hundred years ago, the lines "Musick has Charms
to sooth a savage Breast," and

> Heav'n has no Rage, like Love to Hatred turn'd,
> Nor Hell a Fury, like a Woman scorn'd.

live on as part and parcel of our speech today.

VI

While *The Mourning Bride* was being printed, Congreve received
from Catherine Trotter some commendatory verses to appear with
the play. He wrote a very gracious letter, regretting that it was too
late to include the verses and adding: " . . . all the satisfaction that
I can take, and all the sacrifice that I make to you, is only to stifle
some verses on the same barren subject, which were printed with it,
and now, I assure you, shall never appear, whatever apology I am
forced to make to the authors." The precocious Mrs. Trotter, than
only eighteen, had been writing poems and plays since her early teens
and had already produced one play at Drury Lane. Congreve now

---

[31] Quoted from a letter among the manuscripts of Earl Cowper, Melbourne Hall,
Derbyshire, by the Hist. MSS. Com., *Twelfth Report,* Appendix, Part II, London,
1888, p. 368. Since this letter, dated 16 March 1696/7, says the play "was acted till
Saturday," and since 16 March 1696/7 fell on Tuesday, the Saturday on which *The
Mourning Bride* ended its run of thirteen consecutive days was March 13. By counting
back thirteen days (omitting Sundays) we find that the play had its première on
Saturday, 27 February 1696/7—unless the Lenten season closed the theatres on
Wednesdays and Fridays, in which case the première must have been a week earlier.
[32] *Ibid.*

became her sponsor, assisted in the staging of her next play at Lincoln's Inn Fields, and advised her with her later work.

At this period, it is said, each new play brought on the stage at Lincoln's Inn Fields had to secure first the approbation of Congreve.[33] He was clearly in a position to aid aspiring young dramatists, and he gave his assistance generously. One whom he delighted in helping was Charles Hopkins, son of the Bishop of Derry, who had, like Congreve, been trained at Trinity College, Dublin. Congreve saw three of Hopkins' poetic tragedies produced by his company between 1695 and 1700. For the first—*Pyrrhus, King of Epirus*—Congreve wrote the Prologue. Hopkins dedicated his next play, *Boadicea* (1697), to Congreve, saying that while others may "Court the slippery Friendship of the Great," he preferred the "nobler" address to his friend. He admitted his literary debt to Congreve:

> From you, my Muse her Inspiration drew, . . .
> You taught me first . . .

And then he added:

> Nor does your Verse alone our Passions move,
> Beyond the Poet, we the Person Love.
> In you, and almost only you; we find
> Sublimity of Wit, and Candour of the Mind . . .
> You know my Soul, like yours, without design,
> You know me yours, and I too know you mine.
> I owe you all I am. . . .

Congreve's sponsorship of Catherine Trotter, and more particularly of Mrs. Mary Pix, won for him the hostility of the rival theatre in Drury Lane. Each of these young dramatists gave a first play to the patentees at Drury Lane and then turned to the Betterton group at Lincoln's Inn Fields. This defection could not pass unnoticed and unresented at a time when rivalry between the two dramatic companies was at its height. Much of the resentment was against Congreve, since the young writers had been led away by his reputation, if not by his active solicitation.

During 1697 Congreve's company produced very successfully a comedy by Mrs. Pix entitled *The Innocent Mistress*. This play is a comedy of manners, showing definitely the influence of Congreve.

---

[33] Congreve's responsibility for plays accepted at the Lincoln's Inn Field Theatre is stated specifically in *A Letter to Mr. Congreve on his Pretended Amendments, &c. of Mr. Collier's Short View of the Immorality and Prophaneness of the English Stage* (London, 1698), p. 4.

While her next play was yet in manuscript, so Mrs. Pix declared,[34] George Powell of the Drury Lane group stole the plot for his hastily written play, *The Imposture Defeated*. Congreve naturally sympathized with his aggrieved pupil and went to see Powell's stolen play with no friendly feelings. The limits to which his partisanship reputedly carried him are suggested by an anonymous pamphlet written by one of Powell's friends:

... the mighty Man of Wit ... at the Representation of this Play ... was seen very gravely with his Hat over his Eyes among his chief Actors, and Actresses, together with the two She Things, call'd *Poetesses*, which Write for his House, as 'tis nobly call'd; thus seated in State among those and some other of his Ingenious critical Friends, they fell all together upon a full cry of Damnation, but when they found the malicious Hiss would not take, this very generous, obliging Mr. *Congreve* was heard to say, *We'll find out a New way for this Spark, take my word there is a way of clapping of a Play down*.[35]

The epithets *generous* and *obliging*, even ironically used, give eloquent testimony of the reputation that Congreve had earned.

[34] See the Prologue of her comedy, *The Deceiver Deceived*, acted at Lincoln's Inn Fields Theatre about December, 1697, and published the following year.

[35] *Animadversions on Mr. Congreve's late Answer to Mr. Collier* (London, 1698), pp. 34, 35.

CHAPTER VI

FAREWELL TO THE STAGE

I

SELDOM did Congreve allow anything to disturb the evenness of his temper, to embroil him in controversy. By nature he was composed and diplomatic. Young as he was, his cool head quieted the bickerings of Dryden and Tonson. But for all his complaisance, he could be moved, as in the controversy over *The Double-Dealer*, to lash out against his critics. In the spring of 1698 came an attack that stirred him more deeply than anything else in his career.

The man who made the attack was Jeremy Collier, nonjuring clergyman and controversialist. Born in 1650 and educated at Caius College, Cambridge, he had been given a living in Suffolk. His High-Church stand and sympathy with Catholicism brought him, under James II, appointments as lecturer at Gray's Inn and Preacher of the Rolls. At the time of the Revolution three years later he began a series of pamphlets in favor of James II and stoutly refused to take the oath of allegiance to William and Mary. He continued in London as minister of a nonjuring congregation. His open hostility to the new government led to short terms of imprisonment. Collier throve on the public notice that came to him. He added greatly to his notoriety by giving absolution in a most flamboyant way to the two knights who had been found guilty of plotting the death of King William. With two other nonjuring ministers he boarded the cart on the way to execution. The *Protestant Mercury* for April 3–6, 1696, was quick to point out that giving absolution "openly in the Cart, when it might have been done privately elsewhere, looks like something I will not name." The exasperated government brought the three ministers before the King's Bench, where a true bill was found. Collier may have been fearless enough at other times, but in this instance he slipped away, leaving his two colleagues to stand trial alone.

In his retreat Collier wrote a pamphlet to defend the giving of absolution to the condemned men, and then turned his restless energies to the theatre in an attack which he published in April, 1698, under the title, *A Short View of the Immorality and Profaneness of the English Stage: Together with the Sense of Antiquity upon this Argu-*

62

ment, by Jeremy Collier, M. A.[1] Collier began with relative modera-
tion, as if he had in mind simply a reform of the abuses of the stage,
but before he ended he showed that his real purpose was to destroy
the English theatre entirely. He held the stage responsible for the
melancholy corruption of the age and wanted all theatres shut tight.

The dramatists, for their part, believed that the theatre, instead of
corrupting the age, had merely reflected it. But they were not blind
to the licentiousness of the stage and had already called attention to
the need for reform. In 1686 Dryden had written, in his ode *To the
Pious Memory of . . . Mrs. Anne Killigrew:*

> O gracious God! how far have we
> Profan'd thy heav'nly gift of poesy!
> Made prostitute and profligate the Muse,
> Debas'd to each obscene and impious use,
> Whose harmony was first ordain'd above
> For tongues of angels, and for hymns of love!
> O wretched we! why were we hurried down
>   This lubric and adult'rate age,
> (Nay, added fat pollutions of our own,)
>   T' increase the steaming ordures of the stage?
> What can we say t' excuse our *second fall?*

Only the year before the appearance of the *Short View* Congreve, in
his Dedication to *The Mourning Bride*, had lamented "the licentious
Practice of the Modern Theatre." The dramatists, then, if not actually seeking reform, would probably not have opposed a rational
correction of abuses. When they discovered that Collier's objective
was the destruction of the theatre, they naturally fought back. They
were also annoyed by Collier's lack of artistic sense and judgment,
and angered by the clumsy viciousness of his satire.

Congreve, Dryden, and Vanbrugh bore the brunt of the attack. It
was noted at the time that Collier had "a particular pique against
Mr. Congreve."[2] Why Collier should have had any special bitterness
toward the one of the three least morally offensive is a little puzzling
unless, perhaps, he had taken offense at Congreve's poems in praise

---

[1] Although the Preface is dated March 5, 1697/8, the *Short View* did not appear
until the latter half of April, as is shown by the announcement of publication in *The
Flying Post* for April 19–21, 1698. The Collier controversy is discussed at length by
Gosse and Taylor, in their biographies of Congreve; by Montague Summers, *The
Works of William Congreve*, I, 30–53; by Joseph Wood Krutch, *Comedy and Conscience
after the Restoration* (New York: Columbia University Press, 1924); and elsewhere.

[2] *Some remarks upon Mr. Collier's Defense of his Short View of the English Stage, etc.
In vindication of Mr. Congreve, etc. In a letter to a Friend.* The publication of this
pamphlet was announced by the *Post Man* for December 3–6, 1698.

of King William—a usurper, in Collier's eyes. The *Short View* was being composed, we must remember, at the very period when the author was in hiding from the despised government of King William.

Congreve was slow to enter the lists with the rampant clergyman. He was still young, sensitive to criticism, and inexperienced in the rough-and-ready pamphlet wars of the day. Collier, on the other hand, was forty-eight years old, a seasoned controversialist and pamphleteer, never happier than when in the public eye. The furor caused by the first edition of the *Short View* increased, and a second edition larger than the first was soon called for. Congreve then felt that he must meet the attack, and in July, nearly three months after the *Short View* had first appeared, he issued his *Amendments of Mr. Collier's False and Imperfect Citations, &c.*[3]

In his reply, Congreve lost something of the evenness of his temper and too frequently lowered himself to the plane of his adversary. The depth of his anger is apparent as he writes:

If I do not return his Civilities in calling him Names, it is because I am not very well vers'd in his *Nomenclatures;* therefore for his *Foot pads*, which he calls us in his Preface, and for his *Buffoons* and *Slaves in the Saturnalia*, which he frequently bestows on us in the rest of his Book, I will onely call him Mr. *Collier*, and that I will call him as often as I think he shall deserve it.

Colley Cibber thought that Congreve was "too much hurt" to defend himself effectively. But he was calm enough when he came to lay down the fundamental principles on which he was to base his defense.

Collier had protested against the satirical representation of persons of noble birth. Congreve approached his defense with an appeal to reason. Aristotle, he pointed out, had defined comedy as "an Imitation of the worse sort of People . . . not . . . the worse sort of People in respect to their Quality, but in respect to their Manners," to the end that vicious people may be "made asham'd of their Follies or Faults, by seeing them expos'd in a ridiculous manner." This was answer sufficient for an age which recognized Aristotle as the established authority.

Congreve next contended that by the very nature of comedy the poet must "represent vicious and foolish Characters." But surely, he argued, the author's own sentiments are not to be confounded with those of the foolish persons on the stage any more than "a Painter should be believ'd to resemble all the ugly Faces that he draws." Collier had been guilty of just such a confusion.

Congreve then urged that no passage be judged apart from its

[3] Congreve's *Amendments* was announced in the *Post Man* for July 9–12, 1698.

context—"out of its proper Scene, or alienated from the Character by which it is spoken." "I cannot think it reasonable," he continued, "because Mr. *Collier* is pleas'd to write one Chapter of *Immodesty*, and another of *Profaneness*, that therefore every Expression traduc'd by him under those Heads, shall be condemn'd as obscene and profane immediately, and without any further Enquiry."

Finally, Congreve held that plays should not be condemned simply because of words taken from the Holy Scriptures, without consideration of the use to which the words are put. With his four general principles laid down, Congreve was ready to consider the specific attacks on his plays under each of Collier's four headings—immodesty, profaneness, abuse of the clergy, and encouragement of immorality.

Collier had been troubled by the stage treatment of viscounts and duchesses. He cared little how the lower classes fared. But Congreve, with Aristotle as his authority, yielded nothing of the poet's right to satirize folly and vice wherever found. "When Vice shall be allowed as an Indication of Quality and good Breeding," said Congreve, "then it may also pass for a piece of good Breeding to complement Vice in Quality: But till then, I humbly conceive, that to expose and ridicule it, will altogether do as well."

The *Short View* had attacked at some length the immodesty of a scene between Osmyn and Almeria in *The Mourning Bride*. This play was one that Sir Richard Blackmore, in his Preface to *King Arthur*, had praised for its freedom from "immodest Images or Expressions." "If there be Immodesty in that Tragedy," protested Congreve, "I must confess my self incapable of ever writing any thing with Modesty or Decency." Congreve concluded his defense of the play very effectively:

I confess I have not much to say in Commendation of any thing that I have Written: But if a fair-dealing-man, or a candid Critick had examin'd that Tragedy, I fancy that neither the general Moral contain'd in the two last Lines; nor the several particular Morals interwoven with the success of every principal Character, would have been overseen by him.

Collier had objected to many passages in Congreve's plays on grounds of profanity and had cited the following examples from *The Old Bachelor:*

Vainlove. Could you be content to go to Heav'n?

Bellmour. Hum, not immediately, in my Conscience not Heartily? (III, ii.)

Sharper. *Vainlove*, I have been a kind of a Godfather to you, yonder: I have promised and vow'd some things in your Name, which I think you are bound to perform. (V. xiv.)

"I meant no ill by this Allegory," countered Congreve, "nor do I perceive any in it now. Mr. *Collier* says it was meant for Drollery on the Cathechism; but he has a way of discovering Drollery where it never was intended; and of intending Drollery where it can never be discovered."

Collier had taken exception also to Scandal's determination to "die a Martyr rather than disclaim his Passion," and to Cynthia's observation "that though Marriage makes Man and Wife one Flesh, it leaves them two Fools." Congreve simply denied any idea of jesting upon Scripture, or of treating sacred matters lightly. He very properly called these objections "trifling Cavils."

Finally Congreve lost his self-control over Collier's misreading of *Love for Love.* "*Jeremy* bred at the University? Who told him so? What *Jeremy* does he mean, *Jeremy Collier*, or *Jeremy Fetch?* The last does not any where pretend to have been bred there. And if the t'other would but keep his own Counsel, and not Print *M. A.* on the Title Page of his book, he would be no more suspected of such an Education than his Name-sake." This was a personal thrust at Collier, who liked to display his learning—in the text and also on the title page. To Congreve any display of this sort was repugnant. His *Alma Mater*, Trinity College, Dublin, had conferred upon him the M. A. degree in 1696, but it never appeared on his title pages. He was so modest about the degree that his biographers have hitherto overlooked its existence, and we might now have no knowledge of it except for the record in the minutes of the college.

Congreve the controversialist was never equal to Congreve the artist, but he was at his best in his reply to Collier's plea for reverent treatment of *all* clergymen, regardless of their morals. Congreve insisted that "no Man living" had "greater respect for a good Clergyman" than he. But if a clergyman "is found to play the Knave, he is subject to the Penalties of the Law, equally with the Layman; if he plays the Fool, he is equally with a Lay-fool, the subject of Laughter and Contempt." And he continued:

I know many Reverent Clergymen now living whose Names I cannot hear without Awe and Reverence: And why is that? Not from their Heraldry, but their Humility, their Humanity, their exceeding Learning, which is yet exceeded by their Modesty; their exemplary Behaviour in their whole Lives and Conversations; their Charitable Censures, of Youthful Errors and Negligences, their fatherly and tender Admonitions, accompanyed with all sweetness of Behaviour; and full of mild yet forcible Perswasion.

Many of Collier's accusations were foolish, as Congreve easily demonstrated. But there was also a fundamental element of soundness in Collier's contentions. The stage was sadly in need of reform, as Congreve, in calmer moments, had already admitted. His blanket denial near the end of his defense is entirely too sweeping. No doubt the spirit of the attack had so enraged him that he could not judge clearly and sanely. Before leaving the subject, however, he struck a fairer balance. "I think truly," he wrote, that Collier "had a fair appearance of Right on his side in the Title Page of his Book; but with reason I think I may also affirm, that by his mis-management he has very much weak'ned his Title. He that goes to Law for more than his Right, makes his Pretentions, even to that which is his Right, suspected."

The *Short View* was not a well written or reasonable attack on the abuses of the stage, but it was vigorous and sorely needed, as everybody admitted. The unquestionable timeliness of the book made it a sensation, and the government that had forced Collier into seclusion two years before now thanked him for centering attention on a needed reform. It had no intention, however, of suppressing the stage. Nor did it take seriously Collier's attack on contemporary dramatists as corrupters of the age. It accepted at face value their declared desire for reform. And—what is most revealing—when the next theatrical company was licensed, it was announced in *The London Gazette* for 21–25 December 1704 that the Queen had selected Congreve and Vanbrugh, the two living dramatists most vigorously attacked by Collier, for the management and "for the better Reforming the Abuses and Immorality of the Stage."

II

A popular new play was then desperately needed by the dramatic company in which Congreve was a sharer. The great success of *Love for Love* in 1695, and of *The Mourning Bride* two years later, had been bright spots for the Betterton group. Too many of the plays, as Downes said, "answer'd not the Companys Expectation." Betterton strove to increase his audiences by bringing in fine dancers and singers from Italy; but the great expense left very little profit. As time went on the competition from the rival company in Drury Lane became serious. Some of Betterton's more famous actors were past their prime and losing ground while younger players with the patentees were steadily gaining. Fresh plays by a rising young Irishman named Farquhar were bringing crowded houses to Drury Lane. In the late autumn of 1699 Farquhar's *The Constant Couple* began a sensational run that was very hard on the Betterton group. On Christmas Day Vanbrugh mentioned their desperate state in a letter to the Earl of Manchester: "Matters running very low with 'em this Winter; if Congreve's Play don't help 'em they are undone. 'tis a Comedy and will be play'd about Six weeks hence. nobody has seen it yet."[4]

The six weeks, however, stretched out to ten or twelve. Congreve continued to polish his comedy—he admitted in his Dedication the "care and Pains" he had taken with it—and brought it on the stage early in March. On March 12 Dryden wrote to Mrs. Steward: "Congreve's new play has had but moderate success, though it deserves much better."[5] On the same day Lady Marow wrote to an acquaintance in the country: " 'The way of the World,' Congreve's new play, doth not answer expectation, there being no plot in it but many witty things to ridicule the Chocolate House, and the fantastical part of the world."[6] Downes also thought that the comedy was "too Keen a Satyr" to win general applause.

Congreve was aware of what he had done—and left undone. In his Dedication he stated that he had not written *The Way of the World* to please "that general Taste which seems now to be predominant in the Pallats of our Audience." He had written a play to satisfy his own artistic sense. Only the best judges—and these, Dryden reminds us, are the fewest—could fully understand and appreciate what Congreve had achieved. It was to remain for critics of future generations to hail the play as Congreve's masterpiece, the finest English achievement in the comedy of manners.

At the center of the play stand the lovers—Millamant, of the thousand suitors, and Mirabell, her one man of the thousand. "For a discerning Man," Mirabell admits, he is "somewhat too passionate a Lover; for I like her with all her Faults; nay, like her for her Faults. Her Follies are so natural, or so artful, that they become her; and those Affectations which in another Woman wou'd be odious, serve but to make her more agreeable. I'll tell thee, *Fainall*, she once us'd me with that Insolence, that in Revenge I took her to pieces; sifted her, and separated her Failings; I study'd 'em, and got 'em by Rote. The Catalogue was so large, that I was not without Hopes, one Day or other to hate her heartily: To which end I so us'd my self to think of 'em, that at length, contrary to my Design and Expectation, they gave me ev'ry Hour less and less Disturbance; 'till in a few Days it became habitual to me, to remember 'em without being displeas'd. They are now grown as familiar to me as my own Frailties; and in all probability in a little time longer I shall like 'em as well."

⁴ Vanbrugh's *Works*, ed. Dobrée and Webb, IV, 4.
⁵ *Works*, ed. Scott-Saintsbury, XVIII, 177.
⁶ Hist. MSS. Com., *Dartmouth*, III, 145.

Millamant is unquestionably "a sort of an uncertain Woman." In she comes, "full Sail, with her Fan spread and Streamers out." One minute she is saying, "Well, I won't have you *Mirabell*—I'm resolv'd —I think—You may go—Ha, ha, ha. What wou'd you give, that you cou'd help loving me?" And the next, "Well, after all, there is something very moving in a Lovesick Face. Ha, ha, ha—Well I won't laugh, don't be peevish—Heighho! Now I'll be melancholy, as melancholy as a Watch-light. Well *Mirabell*, if ever you will win me woo me now—Nay, if you are so tedious, fare you well." Before the poor fellow can collect his wits, she is off with the parting injunction to "think of me."

"Think of you!" Mirabell explodes. "To think of a Whirlwind, tho' 'twere in a Whirlwind, were a Case of more steady Contemplation; a very Tranquility of Mind and Mansion. A Fellow that lives in a Windmill, has not a more whimsical Dwelling than the Heart of a Man that is lodg'd in a Woman. There is no Point of the Compass to which they cannot turn, and by which they are not turn'd; and by one as well as another; for Motion not Method is their Occupation. To know this, and yet continue to be in Love, is to be made wise from the Dictates of Reason, and yet persevere to play the Fool by the force of Instinct."

Millamant finally consents to listen to the addresses of her lover: "Ay, if you please, *Foible*, send him away,—Or send him hither,—just as you will, dear *Foible*.—I think I'll see him—Shall I? Ay, let the Wretch come." Then, after that inimitable scene in which Millamant lays down her delightful provisos, she concludes: "These Articles subscrib'd, if I continue to endure you a little longer, I may by degrees dwindle into a Wife."

Congreve declared frankly that artistic values meant more to him than popular applause. He had catered to the favor of the audience in *The Old Bachelor*. But as he looked back over that play his aesthetic conscience rebuked him because he had treated his audience "cheaply" then, and he scorned it for applauding. Even *Love for Love*, much superior to the first comedy, did not satisfy Congreve, and he called the play but "Homely Fare." For *The Way of the World* he made no such apology. In that play, he knew that he had "gain'd a Turn of Stile, or Expression more Correct, or at least more Corrigible."[7] He believed that he had come nearer to his ideal than in any other play, and he might well question whether he could hope to write anything superior. If the audience would not accept it, he could only

---

[7] See the Dedication to *The Way of the World*.

conclude that it would be impossible for him to satisfy both his audience and himself. Should he now drop down from the level that he had reached and prostitute his muse to the lower taste of the town? His decision not to do so remained firm throughout the remainder of his life. He had outgrown the technique of *The Old Bachelor*, and the London audience would not accept the type of high comedy that now satisfied his artistic sense. At the age of thirty, therefore, he decided, as a matter of principle, to write no more for the popular stage.

He made no secret of his decision, nor of his reasons for it. The author of the *Memoirs* (1730), who said that he had known Congreve for "near thirty Years," had "often heard him declare" the reason for his retirement.[8] Many years after Congreve's death, persons who had never known the author of *The Way of the World* began giving other reasons to explain why he had stopped writing for the stage so abruptly while still a young man. The Collier controversy, thought one, "occasioned a dislike" for the stage. This suggestion is refuted by the fact that Congreve went on to write his finest play after the duel with Collier. Another said that "the Easiness of his Circumstances Render'd any Subservience to the Opinions and Caprice of the Town absolutely unnecessary to him,"—forgetting that for years to come (according to Swift) "Congreve scarce could spare a shilling to discharge his chair." Still others make much of the poor state of Congreve's health—without, however, being able to show that it was much worse after 1700 than before. Each of these considerations may have helped to confirm his "strong Resolution" to quit the ungrateful stage. Among others, perhaps, were his natural lassitude and disinclination to risk another "failure." But none of these reasons was adduced by Congreve's contemporaries. Those who knew him were satisfied that his premature withdrawal from active dramatic writing was caused by his desire to preserve his artistic integrity.

III

Although Congreve wrote no more for the professional stage, he continued to express in various ways his interest in theatrical affairs. During the spring of 1701 musical London was keyed up over the

[8] See *Memoirs of the Life, Writings, and Amours of William Congreve* Esq. (London, 1730), p. 11, published under the pseudonym of Charles Wilson. The idea that the Collier controversy led Congreve to quit writing for the stage was first advanced in T. Cibber's *Lives of the Poets* (1753), IV, 90. The influence of Congreve's financial "Easiness" was suggested by David E. Baker, *The Companion to the Play-House* (London, 1764), II, under "Congreve"; also by Walter Harris, *The History of the Writers of Ireland* (Dublin, 1764), p. 294. More recent biographers have hit upon Congreve's poor health as a reason for his early withdrawal from dramatic writing.

production of his masque, *The Judgment of Paris*. As early as March 18–21, 1699/1700, the *London Gazette* had announced a prize competition of the value of two hundred pounds. The leading composers of the day offered musical scores: Godfrey Finger, who had written music for songs in *Love for Love* and *The Mourning Bride;* John Weldon, organist at New College, Oxford; Daniel Purcell, brother of the late great Henry Purcell; and John Eccles, master of the King's Musicians. Each of these composers was to be heard "severally," as Congreve wrote Keally, and then all were to be heard again "in one day, in order to a decision."[9]

The first music, composed by Eccles, was heard at the old Dorset Garden Theatre on Friday, March 21, 1700/1. This showy old playhouse by the Thames had been forsaken at the union of the patentees for the more conveniently located Theatre Royal in Drury Lane. It continued to be, however, the favorite place for operas and plays requiring very elaborate settings. Dorset Garden was well adapted to the staging of Congreve's masque, with its ornate setting on Mount Ida. Here the shepherd Paris is "seated under a Tree, and playing on his Pipe" as "*Mercury* descends with his *Caduceus* in one Hand, and an Apple of Gold in the other." Venus, Pallas, and Juno follow "in several Machines." After the decision falls to Venus, "several *Cupids* descend, the three *Graces* alight from the Chariot of *Venus*, they call the *Howrs*, who assemble; with all the Attendants on *Venus*. All join in a Circle round her, and sing the last grand *Chorus;* while *Juno* and *Pallas* ascend."

Congreve wrote enthusiastically to Keally about the first performance:

Indeed, I don't think any one place in the world can show such an assembly. The number of performers, besides the verse-singers, was 85. The front of the stage was all built into a concave with deal boards; all which was faced

---

[9] For the early stage history of *The Judgment of Paris* see Sir John Hawkins, *A General History of the Science and Practice of Music* (London, 1776), IV, 539, 540; and *Grove's Dictionary of Music and Musicians*, ed. H. C. Calles (New York, 1927–28), under the names of the four composers in the competition. Some of the contemporary notices are in Congreve's letter to Keally dated March 26, 1701, the *London Post* for April 9–11, 1701, and the *Post Boy* for May 31–June 3, 1701. Publication of the masque was announced in the *Post Man* for March 22–25, 1701. George Stepney, Envoy to Vienna, wrote Lord Halifax on December 3–14, 1701 (Bodleian MS. 25, 427, f. 67): "I thank you for your Eccles his Musick, wch. I suppose is got by this time to Hamburgh and will shortly be here, where Finger will see it performed to ye best advantage: He assures me notwithstanding the partiality which was shown by ye Duke of Somerset and others in favor of Welding and Eccles, Mr. Purcell's Musick was the best (I mean after his own, for no Decision can destroy the Love we have for our selves)."

with tin, to increase and throw forwards the sound. It was all hung with sconces of wax-candles, besides the common branches of lights usual in the playhouses. The boxes and pit were all thrown into one; so that all sat in common: and the whole was crammed with beauties and beaux, not one scrub being admitted. The place where formerly the music used to play, between the pit and stage, was turned into White's chocolate-house; the whole family being transplanted thither with chocolate, cool'd drinks, ratafia, portico, &c. which every body that would called for, the whole expence of every thing being defrayed by the subscribers. I think truly the whole thing better worth coming to see than the jubilee.

Congreve was the more enthusiastic because Anne Bracegirdle was Venus. In a postscript to his letter to Keally he added, "Our friend Venus performed to a miracle." It is interesting—and characteristic of the man—that Congreve makes no mention of his own important contribution.

Before the end of March the masque was performed to Finger's music, and during April, to Daniel Purcell's. A little later Weldon had his individual hearing, and then all four of the musical settings were heard one after the other on Tuesday, June 3, 1701. The actors, Doggett and Wilks, who had "farmed" the gallery at Dorset Garden, announced that rates for the final day would be the same as charged for single performances.

The result of the competition was something of a surprise, the first prize of one hundred pounds going to the least known of the composers, the twenty-five-year-old Oxford organist, John Weldon. The reputation he thus gained enabled him to move to London and to write the musical scores for several operas; and on the death of Dr. Blow in 1708, he succeeded as organist at the Royal Chapel. The second prize of fifty pounds went to Eccles, the third of thirty pounds to Purcell, and the fourth of twenty pounds to Finger. For Godfrey Finger the decision was humiliating. Last place in a competition upon which the attention of the English musical world had centered for months was a sore disappointment to one who had been a leading composer since the reign of James II. He was so chagrined that he withdrew from England and returned to his native Germany.

The Judgment of Paris with Weldon's music was performed again at Drury Lane in January, 1704/5; but Weldon's complete musical score was never printed and is now lost, except for the music to Juno's song, "Let ambition fire the mind." Eccles' music was printed and was probably the score used for the revival of the masque in 1745, when the Prince of Wales took the part of Paris. The Eccles score was certainly used for the revival of *The Judgment of Paris* in 1923, at the Cambridge Festival of British Music. Congreve wrote Keally that Eccles' music was "universally admired." He had called on Eccles to score many of the songs in his comedies, and a few months after the performance of *The Judgment of Paris* he turned to him for the music to his ode for St. Cecilia's Day. Later Eccles composed the music to the opera *Semele*, which was printed with Congreve's collected works in 1710. This opera, like the masque, was written years before it was published—possibly soon after the production of *The Judgment of Paris*. It is probable that the opera was never brought on the stage during Congreve's lifetime,[10] though it has had several performances since, with a musical score provided by Handel.

IV

On March 30, 1704, *The Daily Courant* announced "a new Farce, never acted before, call'd *Squire Trelooby*," to be acted at Lincoln's Inn Fields Theatre along with the subscription music provided by the nobility. The farce was a translation of Molière's *Monsieur de Pourceaugnac* made, according to Downes, by Vanbrugh, Congreve, and Walsh. Somehow Joseph Keally in Ireland got the idea that his friend was responsible for the whole, and Congreve had to correct him in his letter of May 20, 1704: "The translation you speak of is not altogether mine; for Vanbrugh and Walsh had a part in it. Each did an act of a French Farce. Mine, and I believe theirs, was done in two mornings; so there can be no great matter in it."

This farce that Congreve mentioned so lightly—though he did admit that "it made people laugh"—was acted by selected players from both houses, including Betterton, Mrs. Bracegirdle, Doggett, and Cibber. Both Mrs. Bracegirdle and Mrs. Leigh chose the play later in the season for their benefit performances; and in 1706, when audiences were thin at the new theatre in the Haymarket, Vanbrugh rewrote one act and gave half a dozen performances. Downes tells us that Doggett acted the part of Trelooby so well that "the whole was highly Applauded."

---

[10] *Egerton's Theatrical Remembrances* (London, 1788), p. 115, states that the opera *Semele* was acted at the Haymarket and printed in quarto in 1707. *A New Theatrical Dictionary* (London, 1792), p. 271, states that the opera was acted and printed in 1707 but omits the name of the theatre. These handbooks are probably in error since the *General Dictionary* (1736), states that *Semele*, though set to music by Eccles, was never performed. Genest records no performance of *Semele* for 1707. The January, 1707, issue of *The Muses Mercury* carried this announcement: "The Opera of Semele, for which we are Indebted to Mr. C———e, is set by Mr. Eccles, and ready to be Practic'd, and from the Excellence of those two Masters, in their several kinds, the Town may well expect to be Charm'd, as much as Poetry and Musick can Charm them."

The translation in which Congreve had a part was never printed. Three weeks after the play was first produced, a voluminous translator named John Ozell published anonymously *Monsieur de Pourceaugnac*, or *Squire Trelooby*. In his Preface Ozell explained in detail that his translation had been forestalled by the one acted; and finding that the acted version was not to be printed, he had adopted the names of characters used in the other translation and was offering his play to the public as the one acted—a procedure he thought justified because both were merely translations from Molière. He was trying to be entirely honest with his readers and at the same time trying to get for the published play the benefit of the popularity of the acted play. Ten years later Ozell carefully reprinted the play in the fourth volume of his complete translation of *The Works of Monsieur de Molière*. In the Dedication he claimed the translation as his own.

Some persons have felt that the play printed anonymously in 1704 was the acted play, which the authors wished to disown.[11] One great difficulty in accepting this view, apart from Ozell's claim, is the statement made by Congreve in writing to Keally just a month after the play was published: " . . . somebody thought it worth his while to translate it again, and print it as it was acted: but if you meet such a thing, I assure you it was none of ours." No one acquainted with the intimacy between Congreve and Keally and with the frankness in the correspondence between the two men could think that Congreve was here trying to deceive his Irish friend.

V

The theatre in Lincoln's Inn Fields in which *Squire Trelooby* was first produced had never been considered more than a makeshift for the Betterton group. Hastily constructed within the walls of a tennis court, it could not be compared to Wren's Theatre Royal in Drury Lane. Betterton could not hope for a continuance of the strong public sympathy that almost assured a successful beginning, nor could he hope for a succession of new plays so actable and appealing as *Love for Love*. The nine years that had passed since Betterton opened his new theatre with Congreve's masterpiece had brought increasing difficulties to the old actor. Most of his players, excellent and justly famous as they were, were getting on in years, while the younger

[11] See Gosse, *Life of Congreve* (New York, 1924), pp. 135–137; Montague Summers, *The Works of William Congreve* (London, 1923), I, 57–59; D. Crane Taylor, *William Congreve* (1931), pp. 181–184; Alwin Thaler in *Representative English Comedies*, IV (New York, 1936), pp. 414, 415. The problem is considered somewhat more at length by the present author in "The Authorship of *Squire Trelooby*," *RES*, VI (1928), 1–10.

actors who had stayed with the patentees, such as Colley Cibber and
Pinkethman, were coning into their maturity. With the addition of
Wilks and Estcourt from Ireland, and with the arrival of Mrs. Oldfield and her rapid rise to popularity, the patentees were in a position
to offer Betterton dangerous competition.

The old theatre in Lincoln's Inn Fields now seemed more than ever
a handicap, and a project was set on foot to build a fine new theatre
for Betterton. By Mindsummer, 1703, Vanbrugh wrote Tonson that
he had purchased for two thousand pounds a site for the theatre in the
Haymarket, and had already drawn the plans. In the same letter he
mentioned going to Hampton Court with Congreve on one evening
and dining with him on the next. The two men were much together,
for they were planning to share in the management of the new theatre.
To raise funds for construction they turned to the noblemen in the
Kit-Cat Club,[12] of which both were members, and secured thirty
subscriptions of one hundred guineas each. One of these subscribers
was the Duke of Newcastle, whose agreement with Vanbrugh, witnessed by Congreve on May 8, 1704,[13] insured him free admission to
the proposed theatre. The cornerstone had been laid during the preceding month by the Duke of Somerset, senior member of the Kit-
Cats.

There was work enough to occupy both of the managers. The supervision of the building of the playhouse naturally fell to Vanbrugh, the
architect. In the meantime Congreve was capitalizing upon his wide
acquaintance among the nobility to secure one-hundred-guinea subscriptions. He was also busily conferring with singers and players
needed for the fine new theatre.[14] The Betterton group, of course,
would form the nucleus, but others would be needed. Among the
recruits were foreign opera singers and half a dozen players enticed
away from the patentees at Drury Lane, including Congreve's old
Dublin friends, Doggett and Bowen.

Congreve was genuinely interested in play production. He took a
large part in the casting and directing of his own plays. After he was
made a full sharer with the Betterton group in 1695, he had additional
incentive for lending his assistance. His friends knew where he might
be found as long as the theatrical season was in progress. In the spring

[12] See Robert J. Allen, "The Kit-Cat Club and the Theatre," *The Review of English
Studies*, VII (1931), 56–61.

[13] This document is preserved at Welbeck Abbey. See Hist. MSS. Com., *Portland*,
II, 185.

[14] Congreve's activities as manager of the Haymarket are shown in the Lord
Chamberlain's papers at the Public Record Office 7/3.

of 1702 Davenant wrote to Tonson: "Pray give my service to Mr. Congreve & desire him to let [me] be remember'd in the dressing room at Lincoln's in fields."[15] This interest made Congreve willing to take a part in the management of the new theatre at the same time that it made him a valuable partner for Vanbrugh.

The prospect of good financial returns also encouraged Congreve's undertaking. Since the production of the *The Mourning Bride* in 1697 he had received no substantial income from his plays, and his share in the Betterton company was no longer profitable. His hopes for political preferment had been repeatedly disappointed. His only dependable income, altogether inadequate for a man in his position, was his small salary as one of the five Licensers for Hackney Coaches. The future of the fine new theatre seemed promising, and the managership a very good means of adding to his income.

Congreve found himself absorbed in plans for the new theatre. "I have a multitude of affairs," he wrote Keally in the autumn of 1704. His vacation in the country during the summer had made him fat, he said, almost too fat to buckle his shoe; but keeping pace with his energetic fellow manager would help him to reduce—a thing he was determined to do. The following February he wrote: "I have been so employed, and am still like to be so, that I have no time for any thing. I know not when the house will open, nor what we shall begin withal; but I believe with no opera. There is nothing settled yet." He was indeed busy. For months Keally's Irish friend, the artist Hugh Howard, had been trying to paint Congreve's picture, but Congreve was too busy for the necessary sittings.

One of the "multitude of affairs" was the "License for a New Company of Comedians," which was granted by the Queen on December 14, 1704, to "*Our Trusty and Welbeloved* John Vanbrugh and William Congreve *Esq*."[16] Betterton now gave up his old license and with his whole company began acting under the direction of Vanbrugh and Congreve.

The new playhouse was named the Queen's Theatre in honor of Queen Anne, but it was commonly called the Haymarket Theatre on account of its location. Although it was not entirely finished, it was opened on April 9, 1705, with a foreign opera. Congreve's surmise —and apparently his hope—that the house would open with no opera had not come true. The performers were singers newly arrived from Italy—"the worst that e'er came from thence," says Downes—and the opera continued only a few days to thin houses. Then followed

[15] Transcribed from the original manuscript at Bayfordbury, Hertfordshire.
[16] *The London Gazette* for December 21–25, 1704.

stock plays interspersed with several new ones, but nothing had even
a fair run. At the end of June the managers were glad to bring their
short season to a close with three performances of *Love for Love*.
In February the managers had been confident enough of the success
of the new house to advertise the old playhouse in Lincoln's Inn
Fields for sale or lease. But after three months' trial they were glad
to announce "That the Company will continue to Act at the Theatre
in Little-Lincoln's Inn Fields till Her Majesty's Theatre in the Haymarket be entirely finished."[17]

The dismal failure of the new theatre had been due partly to the
location. The Haymarket, a mile west of Drury Lane and Lincoln's
Inn Fields, was not within easy walking distance of the Inns of
Court. In 1705 many of the fashionable squares that were soon to de-
velop around the Haymarket were "all but so many green Fields of
Pasture, from whence," writes Cibber, the theatre "could draw little
or no Sustenance, unless it were that of a Milk-Diet." But even more
serious than the location was the defect in the acoustics of the new
building. "For what," asks Cibber, "could their vast Columns, their
gilded Cornices, their immoderate high Roofs avail, when scarce one
Word in ten could be distinctly heard in it?" Vanbrugh's semi-oval
arches and high ceilings "occasion'd such an Undulation from the
Voice of every Actor, that generally what they said sounded like the
Gabbling of so many People in the lofty Isles in a Cathedral—The
Tone of a Trumpet, or the Swell of an Eunuch's holding Note, 'tis
true, might be sweeten'd by it, but the articulate Sounds of a speaking Voice were Drown'd by the hollow Reverberations of one Word
upon another."

Congreve was not by nature a man of affairs. The many tedious
details that called for attention soon tired him. He was, moreover, a
man of peace, and therefore troubled by the difficult decisions and the
perverse bickerings which no theatrical manager could long escape.
He did not, like the unscrupulous Rich at Drury Lane, thrive on such
a way of living. Before the end of the year he had given over the
management entirely to Vanbrugh. In the middle of December he
wrote to Keally: "I have quitted the affair of the Haymarket. You
may imagine I got nothing by it: but when I was dipt, and asked
myself, *Quid agam?* replies Terence, *Quid, nisi ut ti redimas captum
quam queas minimo, si nequeas paululo, et quanti queas.*"

[17] The advertisement for sale of L. I. F. appeared in the *London Gazette* for February
19–22, 1705; the later announcement in the *Daily Courant* for July 20, 1705.

CHAPTER VII

AT HOME IN THE STRAND

I

THE Strand had known many centuries of English life before Congreve came to live there. Along this main thoroughfare from the City to the King's palace in Westminster, once each year the King paraded to meet the Lord Mayor of London at Temple Bar and to receive from him the key to the City.

The Strand was what its name implied—the street along the river. But it was far enough away to leave ample space for palatial homes with comfortable gardens that stretched back to the Thames. In the days of Queen Elizabeth this mile's length of the Strand hedged in the town houses of the greatest names in church and state. There lived the Bishops of Carlisle and Bath, as well as the Archbishop of York. There Lord Burghley resided at Exeter House. There the palace formerly used by the Bishop of Durham was granted by the Queen to Sir Walter Raleigh. And another favorite, the Earl of Essex, was a resident of Essex House in the very shadow of the Middle Temple.

Most of these Elizabethan palaces had disappeared before Congreve came up to London in 1689.[1] Somerset House and the Savoy still remained, but many of the fine old houses had given way to short residential streets running north and south. It was here, first in Arundel Street and later in Surrey Street, that Congreve was to make his home for nearly forty years. These streets were connected, midway between the Strand and the river, by tiny Howard Street. Here Anne Bracegirdle lived, a close neighbor to Congreve.[2]

When Congreve began the study of law early in 1691, he naturally lived near the Middle Temple. He did not have chambers within the Temple itself; nor did Joseph Keally, who came a year or two after

[1] For a description of the Strand in Congreve's day see John Macky, *A Journey through England* (London, 1724), I, 171 ff.; John Gay, *Trivia*, II, 11. 477 ff.

[2] Anne Bracegirdle's ownership of the house where she lived in Howard Street is attested by the Rate Books preserved at the Westminster City Hall. Congreve's London residences are indicated by his letters. Joseph Spence, *Anecdotes*, ed. Singer (1820), p. 376, was evidently mistaken in saying that Congreve "lived in the same street" with Mrs. Bracegirdle, but he was her near neighbor.

Congreve.[3] Apparently these old schoolfellows, friends since their years at Kilkenny, secured lodgings together. After three or four years, Congreve's distaste for the law had weaned him away from the Temple, but not from his friend or from his interest in his friend's career. By 1700 Keally went away to practice law in Dublin. Congreve's letters to him repeatedly mention common friends at their old lodgings. "Our friends in Arundel-street" are remembered in one; in another he writes, "All Arundel-street is much yours, and hears of your designs with pleasure. . . . Pray send me word when you are just coming, and make haste."[4] Congreve looked forward eagerly to Keally's return to London and, for his part, planned several return visits to Ireland. Keally could always depend upon Congreve to do his errands in London, whether it was to superintend the grinding of precious stones for a favored young lady or to carry a mesage to the Lord Lieutenant.

It may have been the convenience of the location that kept Congreve year in, year out in the Strand. A short walk from his lodgings brought him to the Inns of Court, to the office of the Licensers for Hackney Coaches, to the theatres, or to his favorite coffeehouses and taverns. In the Strand itself, just west of Somerset House, stood the Fountain Tavern, weekly meeting place of his Kit-Cat Club. North of the Strand, conveniently near in Lincoln's Inn Fields, was the theatre in which Congreve "shared" with Betterton and Anne Bracegirdle, and in which he spent much time aiding in the casting and producing of plays. Near-by in Drury Lane stood the Theatre Royal. A few steps beyond, toward Covent Garden, rose Will's Coffeehouse, in whose large upper room Congreve sat near the master in the circle of Dryden.

During his first ten or twelve years in London Congreve lived the typical life of the gentleman about town.[5] He probably rose and breakfasted about nine and proceeded to make a morning call on a friend or to wait at some nobleman's levee. By noon he would be at the coffeehouse conversing with the wits before taking the air in St. James's Park to meet the ladies. Or, if the weather prevented, he could stay on at the coffeehouse at cards and talk until the two o'clock

[3] The Middle Temple *Admissions to House and Chambers, 1658–1695*, preserved in manuscript at the Library of the Middle Temple, shows that neither Congreve nor Keally was admitted to chambers. It is possible, of course, that they could have resided within the Temple as sub-tenants of some member who had chambers.

[4] See the letters to Keally dated December 10, 1700, January 28, 1700/1, June 7, 1701, etc.

[5] John Macky, *A Journey through England*, I, 162 ff., gives the daily routine of a gentleman in London at the beginning of the eighteenth century.

dinner hour. Then he would make one of a party to dine at a convenient tavern, unless he happened to be invited to the home of a friend. Congreve had many invitations. Swift found him dining in private homes more frequently than in taverns. Dinner over, the next move was to the play, and after that to the upper room at Will's to sup and talk with Dryden and other friends till midnight. But on many an evening, no doubt, he would go instead to pay his devoirs to the ladies at one of the frequent assemblies.

After Dryden's death in 1700, Congreve cared less and less for the society of the wits. His enthusiasm for the hearty life at the coffeehouses, so evident in his letters about 1695, waned after the turn of the century. He lived in comparative retirement near his associates in the Strand, or with close friends at watering places and country houses. In 1700 he wrote Keally that he did not intend to make many friendships. A few close friends he could never see enough of, but casual acquaintances at coffeehouse and at court were burdensome. He felt uncomfortable at being looked upon as the "Great Mr. Congreve." He mentioned his works in the most modest way. He hated to be lionized. He was happiest in the company of a few people to whom he was simply "Will" Congreve, an old acquaintance.

In the summer of 1706 Congreve moved from Arundel Street to Surrey Street.[6] He was to keep his new lodgings for the remainder of his life. He found it pleasant to live with Edward Porter and Mrs. Porter, the actress. With them he had already formed a close friendship, so that he included them in his intimate correspondence. While he was visiting the Continent for a few months in 1700, he enclosed with a letter to Edward Porter a chatty note for Mrs. Porter:

I leave you to Judge whither Holland can be said to be wanting in Gallantry, when it is Customary there to enclose a Billet doux to a Lady, in a letter to her husband . . . for my part I keep the Commandments, I love my neighbor as my selfe, & to avoid Coveting my neighbor's wife I desire to be coveted by her; which you know is quite another thing. . . . I would have written to y^r Mother but that I have changed my religion twice since I left england, & am at present so unsettled, that I think it fit to fix before I endeavour to convert her to my opinion. . . .

Hard times often came upon the players. In such emergencies thrifty Mrs. Porter eked out the family income with small sums earned by sewing. Congreve took it upon himself to put employment in her way. Joseph Keally, prosperous lawyer in Dublin, needed shirts. Mrs. Porter needed work. Congreve assisted both, first by se-

[6] See Congreve's letter to Keally, 26 June 1706.

curing the linen for his friend, and then by sending with one of his many letters to Keally the sempstress' bill, along with praise of Mrs. Porter's skill in producing eleven shirts from "a piece of holland ordinarily making ten."[7]

II

Hard times came home to Congreve. After 1700 his income from playwriting ceased and his profits from Lincoln's Inn Fields Theatre were greatly curtailed. The small audiences that made it impossible for old Betterton to pay his actors made Congreve's share in the Company almost worthless. There was good reason why Congreve could serve Swift only "nasty white wine."[8] He needed every shilling to support his modest way of living.

Congreve had been hoping since 1695 for a lucrative government post. He was still to wait many years. In the meantime, for short periods, he filled two minor offices. In 1697 he served as one of the managers of the Malt Lottery. This lottery, like the Million Lottery that had preceded it, was a scheme for raising taxes, and required, as the managers said, a great deal of "Figureing and examining."[9] The managers tried in various ways to make a success of their work, even going so far as to deny "themselves Coatch hyre att 5s p diem. dinners &c." But the scheme was not successful, and the Lords of the Treasury gave them but half the two hundred pounds allotted to the directors of the Million Lottery. This discrimination seemed unjust to Congreve, after he had denied himself the good "dinners." With five of his fellows he joined in protest—and perhaps his hand is to be seen in the wording of the final item of their memorial: "Lastly, even the unsuccessfullness of the affaire ought to be noe arguemt. against theire Services. The Pooreness of the Mine affording noe pretense against the paymt. of the Labourers." But the Lords of the Treasury were not impressed; they wrote across the back of the petition: "Adhere to ye former resolucõn."

The management of the Malt Lottery was only a temporary appointment, and Congreve hoped for something more permanent. The month following his assignment to the Malt Lottery, Luttrell an-

[7] Congreve to Keally, 2 November 1711.

[8] *Journal to Stella*, 16 February 1710/11.

[9] From the Memorial of the Commissioners of the Malt Lottery, P. R. O., Treasury Papers, T. 1, Vol. 50, No. 43. For the act providing for the Malt Lottery, see *The Statutes of the Realm (1695-1701)* (London, 1830), VII, 247–257. Congreve was one of the eleven commissioners for whom the royal warrant was issued on 23 April 1697. See P. R. O., Treasury Papers, King's Warrant Book XIX, 245, 246; also *Money Book* XIV, 138; *Order Book* IV, 484; *Treasury Minute Book* X, 103, 211.

nounced that he was to be one of the commissioners for "Hawkers and Pedlars."[10] But Congreve did not actually get the appointment. This was probably one of those experiences which he was to remember a few years later when he was lamenting the "fair promises" which had led to disappointment. Indeed he received nothing to augment his income till 1700, when he was given the minor sinecure post of "Customer" at Poole. The annual salary of forty-eight pounds he had to share with the resident deputy. And he lost this position at the end of 1703.[11] In 1704 he found himself, as regards political preferment, just where he had been in 1695. Notwithstanding many fair promises, he still had only the half-salary post of Commissioner for Hackney Coaches, and he was worried lest the changing political front might deprive him even of that. This situation probably explained his willingness to join Vanbrugh in the management of the Haymarket Theatre, then being constructed from Vanbrugh's plans. Business at best was distasteful to Congreve, a thing to be avoided. And theatrical management, as we have seen, proved unusually vexatious and disappointing.

Congreve was not, like his friend Keally, a man of affairs. For Keally, the period at the Middle Temple was one of real preparation for the law. He gained admission to the bar in Dublin. Later he was elected Recorder of Kilkenny and attorney-general of the county Palatine of Tipperary, and he represented Doneraile in the Irish Parliament. Congreve looked forward confidently to the time when his friend would become a judge, as he probably would have but for his premature death in 1713. Keally was going into politics with a gusto that Congreve could not understand. "I find you are resolved," Congreve wrote, "to be a man of this world, which I am sorry for, because it will deprive me of you."[12] As Keally secured one office after another,

[10] *A Brief Historical Relation of State Affairs*, IV, 220. Probably we may accept Luttrell's statement as evidence for a proposed assignment that was never actually made. The Declared Accounts of the Commissioners for Hawkers and Pedlars at the Public Record Office make it certain that Congreve was not one of the Commissioners.

[11] The warrant for letters patent to William Congreve as customer at Poole is dated 3 July 1703 (Treasury Out Letters—Customs and Excise, T. 11. 14, p. 86), and the enrollment was made 1 August 1703 (Patent Roll 3416, 12 William III, Part III, No. 6). On the death of William III, the appointment was renewed (Treasury Minute Book, T. 29. 13, p. 191; Patent Roll 3425, 1 Anne, Part II, No. 38). On the last day of December, 1703, were enrolled the letters patent constituting William Swanton customer in place of Congreve (Patent Roll 3438, 2 Anne, Part I, No. 20). For the salary see the Quarterly Treasury Accounts, General, T. 31. 1, p. 73, and reports for other quarters during Congreve's tenure of office; for the payment of the deputy, see Customs Establishment, Customs 18. 61, under "Poole."

[12] From the letter dated 14 October 1704 (XIII). In a letter to Keally during the

William Congreve.

THE GOVERNMENT OFFICIAL

he tried to put something in the way of his friend. But Congreve was too discouraged to follow up Keally's repeated suggestions concerning ways and means whereby Congreve might get a commissionership. "You may imagine I would not omit such an advantage," Congreve replied, "if it were practicable; but I know it is vain, notwithstanding all the fair promises I have had; for I have not obtained a less matter which I ask'd for. I must have patience; and I think I have. Of my philosophy I make some use."[13]

After Addison had secured a lucrative secretaryship in Ireland, Keally suggested an Irish post for Congreve, only to get another half-hearted reply: "The hint you give me is very kind, and need not seem unfeasible to any who does not know particular persons and circumstances as well as myself."[14] He added that he would really not care for the office except that it would enable him to see Keally. Then he made a confession that may account for the slowness of his advancement: "Ease and quiet is what I hunt after. If I have not ambition, I have other passions more easily gratified." The whole idea of seeking government office was repugnant to him, and also the publicity that such employment entailed. The fame he had won by his plays had not accustomed him to publicity; he could get no pleasure from it. He did not even care to mingle with the larger groups of his own acquaintances. "You know I need not be very much alone," he wrote Keally; "but I choose it, rather than to conform myself to the manners of my court or chocolate-house acquaintance."[15] What he enjoyed and could never get enough of was the intimate companionship of "the few people that I love."[16] A man with such tastes could not follow a political career with any enthusiasm. It was not his way. He was not quite tough enough to go along with his genial Irish friend.

Though Congreve lacked enthusiasm in working for his own political advancement, he gladly helped Keally. His literary prominence and his membership in the Kit-Cat Club had made him acquainted with the political leaders of the day. Not ambitious personally, he had an easy association with them not possible to Keally; and so he could gain hearings for him that otherwise would have been difficult. When Congreve, on a mission from Keally, could not reach the Duke of Ormond at his home, he took advantage of a chance meeting at court.[17]

---

following year (15 December 1705, but generally misdated 1708), Congreve spoke of his friend as "Judge *in futuro*, already in wisdom, gravity, and understanding."

[13] 12 February 1703/4.
[14] 29 November 1708.   [15] 2 July 1700.
[16] Congreve to Keally, 12 February 1703/4.
[17] Congreve to Keally, 20 May 1704.

With the ladies he was even more successful, being able, for example, to arrange for Keally an appointment with Lady Wharton, wife of the Irish Lord Lieutenant.[18] If Congreve had worked as boldly for his own promotion as for that of this friend, he would not have spent the larger part of his life in "one poor office."

At the close of 1705 Congreve became commissioner for wines instead of hackney coaches.[19] There was a certain fitness, and poetic justice at long last, in this new appointment. In his college days Congreve had been one of the best customers of the cellar in the old quadrangle of Trinity. When he was on a Continental trip, nothing stirred him to greater enthusiasm than the "Admirable Champagn" and the "good Burgundy." In preparation for his return to England, he urged Mrs. Porter to put in a supply of "good wine, for I have much to say to you over a bottle underground: & I hope within 3 weeks to satisfie you that no man upon the face of the earth nor in the Cellar" is a more faithful friend. Even a present of cider from Tonson was enough to make him "poke out" a letter to the old publisher. Some Irish usquebaugh sent over by Keally was the subject for several letters, first in pleasant anticipation, then in fear lest the precious usquebaugh had been lost, and finally in overflowing gratitude to the lady who brought it:

. . . no leisure will ever afford me time enough to acknowledge the goodness of that lady (who has not her equal), in remembering one, only considerable in being her creature. I am sure she means the usquebaugh should do me good; and in order to that, I am sure it will be more a cordial, and consequently more effectual, by coming with her, than if sent by any thing alive.[20]

But such joy does not last forever. The year before his appointment as licenser of wines, Congreve was lamenting the scarcity of good wine

[18] See the manuscript letter (undated but probably written in March, 1710) from Congreve to Keally, in the Morgan Library, New York.

[19] Congreve was one of the five "Commissioners and Agents for granting Licenses for Selling Offering by Retail, all and every or any kind of Wine or Wines whatsoever in any City, Town, or place within the Kingdom of England, Dominion of Wales and Town of Berwick upon Tweed, being appointed to ye said Office by Letters Patents under the Greate Seale of England bearing date the XXVIth day of December . . . 1705 . . . during Her Majesty's pleasure. . . . And to Each of them a yearly Salary of Two hundred pounds . . ." (P. R. O., Declared Accounts for the two years ending at Christmas, 1707). The Declared Accounts show that Congreve continued in office at the same salary until 21 December 1714. The Commissioners had ten assistants to carry on the business of the office. See the Treasury Registers—Various, Abstracts of Divers Establishments, P. R. O., T. 48. 1, p. 1.

[20] 2 August 1708. For other comments on wine, see Congreve's letters to the Porters, 11 August 1700 and 27 September 1700; also letters to Keally, 30 April 1706 and 2 March 1707/8.

in London. His appointment, one might think, would have eased conditions, at least in so far as Congreve was concerned. It did not. A few months after he began his duties as licenser, he complained to Keally, "If I have the spleen, it is because this town affords not one drop of wine out of a private house."

Throughout the early years of Queen Anne's reign political affairs were in "very whimsical circumstances."[21] Occasionally hopeful, as Congreve was when he wrote that "affairs begin to look as if they would mend," he was more frequently troubled with "business . . . full of vexation, and without any good consequence." To Keally he admitted that he had lost confidence in his patrons: "How my friends, as you call 'em, mean to proceed in relation to me, I know not yet. They speak as they used to do, and may consequently do as they used to do." He did not allow himself to become too hopeful when the Whigs seemed to entrench themselves more firmly in 1708. And it was just as well for him perhaps, that he did not get the more important post half promised him, for such promotion would have made him a sure target for the Tories two years later.

In the summer of 1710 the political situation changed. Congreve foresaw the downfall of his party. Early in June, before Queen Anne began definitely to break with the Whigs by dismissing Sunderland, Congreve wrote to Keally: "I am weary of the town and politics. . . . If you would have my own private sentiments, I will own I expect nothing that will please me." He was so discouraged and in such poor health that he retired to Richmond to drink spa water and to live quietly all summer long.

Before the summer had ended, many of the Whigs had been dismissed from the Queen's government. At first Congreve confessed himself amazed, unable "to make any conjecture of what is intended by the proceedings at court." Before long the meaning was only too clear, and the significance was brought home to Congreve as Addison and other friends began to lose their civil employments. For Congreve, the situation was serious. He had inherited no fortune, the receipts from his plays had barely satisfied the needs of the period in which they were written, and the income from his civil service was meagre. The emoluments of his "little office"[22] did not provide many luxuries. As his good friend Swift knew,

[21] For Congreve's comments on the political outlook see his letters to Keally, 2 March 1707/8, 12 May 1708, 9 December 1704, 26 June 1706, 6 June 1710, and 10 August 1710.

[22] So described by Lord Halifax (referring to Congreve's office as licenser of wines) in a letter dated 25 April 1712, MSS. of the Duke of Portland, Welbeck Abbey.

Congreve scarce could spare
A shilling to discharge his chair.[23]

Fortune, however, was not wholly unkind. The fact that Congreve
a Whig, was able to retain office throughout the Tory regime at the
end of Queen Anne's reign has often been cited as proof of his mild
party spirit. On the contrary, the correspondence with Keally shows
that he felt very keenly the success or failure of the Whigs. But it was
not in his nature to speak out rashly. He felt, as he expressed it, "very
sensibly and silently,"[24] and he was less objectionable to the Tories
than many a less loyal but more voluble Whig.

The truth of it is that Congreve's office was not important enough
to excite the cupidity of prominent Tories. The yearly salary for licensing wines was twice that of the earlier position, but it was correctly enough described in Lord Halifax's remark concerning Congreve's "little office." The meagreness of Congreve's governmental pay
during the first twenty years, 1695-1714, is emphasized by the income
of Addison for his government service. In 1710 Addison lost one post
that paid two thousand pounds yearly and still held another that
paid twice the income of Congreve's office. In fact, Congreve's total
income for his first twenty years of civil service was but little more
than that of Addison's government pay for a single year.[25]

The relative insignificance of Congreve's office made it possible for
his friends to prevent his dismissal. Swift knew the danger Congreve
was in and commended him to the Tory Lord Treasurer, Robert
Harley. Lord Halifax also appealed to Harley in Congreve's behalf,
once in 1712 when the commission was being changed, and again two
years later when there were rumors of another change.[26] No doubt
Swift, a trusted adviser who was with Harley almost daily, was more
influential than the former Lord Treasurer. Even so, in spite of as-
surances by Swift and Halifax, disturbing rumors of his approaching
dismissal kept reaching Congreve. It was St. John's avowed policy

[23] From Swift's poem entitled "A Libel on the Reverend Dr. Delany, and His
Excellency John, Lord Carteret."

[24] Congreve to Keally, 8 June 1706.

[25] Emoluments of Addison's political offices are shown by Addison's letter to Mr.
Wortley, 21 July 1711. See *The Works of Joseph Addison*, ed. Richard Hurd (London,
1856), V, 401. For a discussion of Congreve's income from political offices see John C.
Hodges, "William Congreve in the Government Service," *Modern Philology*, XXVII
(1929), 183–192.

[26] For appeals made in behalf of Congreve see *The Journal to Stella*, June 22, 30,
July 2, 10, 1711, and December 27, 1712; also the letters from Lord Halifax to the
Earl of Oxford, 25 April 1712 and 13 May 1714, among the MSS. of the Duke of
Portland at Welbeck Abbey.

"to fill the employments of the kingdom down to the meanest with tories";[27] and St. John's influence was becoming more and more important. Only the death of the Queen and the return of the Whigs to power kept Congreve in his post.

Throughout the long period before 1710, while his Whig friends were in a position to do something really handsome for him, Congreve was often bitter at the many "fair promises" left unfulfilled. But he did not, like some of the other wits, allow his disappointments to carry him over to the side of the triumphant Tories. He was much less active, much less voluble, than most of the literary office holders. He was also more consistently loyal than most of them.

III

Congreve's letters during the early years of the eighteenth century reveal that he was full of worries. He had worries not only about finances and disappointments over promised government jobs, but something more vital—worry over his relations with Anne Bracegirdle, which were becoming strained. Their relations had been an integral part of Congreve's life for ten years. He had made no attempt to conceal his delight in her. He had seen her often in private and in public. He had ridden and dined with her "almost every day."

It was small wonder then that Congreve was not only embarrassed but hurt when his cousin, Robert Leke, the third Earl of Scarsdale, laid siege to the lady. The public knew of the Earl's infatuation and tittered over the turn of affairs:

> Do not, most fragrant Earl, disclaim
> Thy bright, thy reputable Flame
>   To *Bracegirdle* the Brown;
> But publicly espouse the Dame,
>   And say G— D— the Town.[28]

Although Lord Scarsdale did not take this advice, his will written on 9 January 1702/3 reveals the seriousness of his interest in the charming actress: "To Mrs. Anne Bracegirdle I give and bequeath one thousand pounds . . . Scarsdale . . . I desire that this Legacy may be the first Money paid."[29] There is preserved in Congreve's own

---

[27] I. S. Leadam, *The History of England from the Accession of Anne to the Death of George II* (London, 1909), p. 181.

[28] From "The Lord Griffin to the Earl of Scarscale," *The Works of Nicholas Rowe, Esq.* (London, 1747), II, 307.

[29] See the will at Somerset House, London, P. C. C., Barrett 20. Lord Scarsdale died at his house in Duke Street on 27 December 1707 and was buried in Westminster Abbey on 4 January 1707/8. See J. L. Chester, *The Marriage, Baptismal, and Burial Register of . . . Westminster* (London, 1876), pp. 261, 262. The will was proved 2 January 1707/8.

handwriting a hitherto unpublished poem which may possibly indicate how Congreve was affected by Anne's inconstancy:

> False tho' you've been to me and Love,
>   I nere can take revenge,
> (So much your wondrous beautys move)
>   Tho' I resent your change.
>
> In hours of bliss we oft have met,
>   They could not allways last;
> And tho' the present I regret,
>   I still am Gratefull for the past.
>
> But think not, Iris, tho' my breast
>   A gen'rous flame has warm'd
> You ere again could make me blest,
>   Or charm as once you charm'd.
>
> Who may your future favours own
>   May future change forgive;
> In Love, the first deceit alone
>   Is what you never can retrieve.[30]

Loyalty to his friends, however, was inherent in Congreve. He bore no malice, and he was to maintain his friendship with Mrs. Bracegirdle to the end of his life. Still "Gratefull for the past," he left her as a token of his regard a bequest of two hundred pounds. In point of fact, she needed no endowment from Congreve. Twenty years before his death, Anne was able to retire from the stage. With the addition of Lord Scarsdale's legacy in 1708, she had ample funds and refused "most advantageous"[31] offers to induce her to return to her profession.

For many years Mrs. Bracegirdle lived on in easy retirement at her house in Howard Street, visited and patronized by the wits of the age. On May 26, 1742, Horace Walpole entertained her for breakfast. "As

---

[30] These four quatrains are apparently the only literary work of Congreve preserved in his own handwriting. The first two quatrains, in a version somewhat less personal, were published by Congreve in his collected *Poems upon Several Occasions*, London, 1710. The last two are now printed for the first time. A careful examination of the manuscript (see the facsimile opposite) shows that Congreve originally wrote the version consisting of the first two stanzas published in 1710 (except that the printed poem shortens "I still am" to "I'm"); then he altered that version by substituting the second person for the third and by changing a few phrases. The third and fourth stanzas, it will be noted, are in the personal tone of the altered version. For permission to reproduce Congreve's manuscript I am indebted to the kindness of Mr. Oliver W. Barrett, who has placed the original in a collection of manuscripts which he has made for his son, Mr. Roger W. Barrett, of Kenilworth, Illinois.

[31] See Cibber's *Apology*, I, 174.

she went out, and wanted her clogs," wrote Walpole, "she turned to me, and said, 'I remember at the playhouse, they used to call Mrs. Oldfield's chair! Mrs. Barry's clogs! and Mrs. Bracegirdle's pattens!' "[32] Earlier in the same year David Garrick had appeared as Bayes in *The Rehearsal* to the general satisfaction of the audience. As a group of visitors was gathered in Howard Street, Colley Cibber spoke disparagingly of Garrick, whom Mrs. Bracegirdle had not yet seen. "The old actress," we are told, "tapped Colley with her fan; 'Come, come, Cibber,' she remarked; 'tell me if there is not something like envy in your character of this young gentleman. The actor who pleases everybody must be a man of merit.' Colley smiled, tapped his box, took a pinch, and, catching the generosity of the lady, replied: 'Faith, Bracey, I believe you are right; the young fellow *is* clever!' "[33]

IV

Congreve lightened his cares and disappointments by writing an occasional poem or essay. In 1701 he furnished to the London Musical Society an ode for the celebration of St. Cecilia's Day. This was a so-called Pindaric ode, a formless monstrosity made popular by Cowley. In the hands of genius, to be sure, it might be molded into an *Alexander's Feast*, but it was no safe tool for a Shadwell or a Tate. Congreve later made a study of the true Greek ode and published, in 1706, his *Discourse on the Pindaric Ode*, explaining the metrical principles so rigidly observed by Pindar. Congreve has been credited justly with the reform of the false Pindaric ode. He was not the first to call attention to the widespread abuse of the form, but he was the first with enough prestige to get a hearing.

Political events in England and the military campaigns on the Continent provided excellent material for light ballads. Congreve read with keen interest of the defeat of the French in the Battle of Oudenarde on 11 July 1708 and hastily celebrated the Allied victory in "Jack French-Man's Defeat:"

> Ye Commons and Peers,
> Pray lend me your Ears,
> I'll sing you a Song if I can;
> How *Louis le Grand*
> Was put to a Stand,
> By the Arms of our Gracious Queen *Anne*

---

[32] *Letters*, ed. Toynbee, I, 229.
[33] Doran's *Annals of the English Stage*, ed. R. W. Lowe (London, 1888), I, 169.

Fourteen stanzas in this swinging metre narrate the prowess of the English and the ignoble flight of the Pretender after watching the battle from a church steeple.

> Not so did behave
> The Young *Hannover* Brave
> In this Bloody Field I assure you;
> When his War-Horse was shot
> Yet He matter'd it not,
> But Charg'd still on Foot like a Fury.

Published as a broadside, the ballad became immediately popular. The next year it was included, along with a Latin translation, in Tonson's *Sixth Miscellany*. The translation was the work of Joseph Keally, as we may infer from Congreve's letter of 9 November 1708: "I thank you for the Latin ballad: I think it is as well as the thing will bear." Congreve considered the piece so trivial that he never allowed his name to appear with the printed ballad. The authorship, however, is made certain by a reference in the diary of Mary Clavering, Countess Cowper, one of the "toasts" of Congreve and his fellow Kit-Cats:

I told him [the Prince of Wales] that before his coming hither, I and my Children had constantly drunk his Health by the Name of *Young Hanover Brave*, which was the Title Mr. *Congreve* had given him in a Ballad. This made him ask who Mr. *Congreve* was, and so gave me an Opportunity of saying all the Good of Mr. *Congreve* which I think he truly deserves.[34]

Congreve wrote and collected ballads throughout his life. He wrote his "Buxom Joan of Deptford" several years before Sailor Ben sang it in *Love for Love*,[35] and he supplied the doggerel ballad on quadrille for the *Miscellany* of Swift and Pope only a year or two before his death. Since Congreve did not consider his own ballads worth collecting and preserving, we shall never know how many he wrote.

Congreve was also careless about preserving his miscellaneous essays. By the merest chance we learn that he was the author of one of the additional *Tatlers* (for February 20, 1710/11) published by Harrison. After spending the evening of February 13, 1710/11, with Congreve, Swift wrote in his *Journal* to Stella:

[34] *Diary of Mary, Countess Cowper, Lady of the Bedchamber to the Princess of Wales, 1714–1720* (London, 1864), pp. 23, 24 (November, 1714). See also F. Elrington Ball, "Congreve as a Ballad-Writer," *N & Q*, Ser. 12, VIII (1921), 301–303.

[35] The broadside has six stanzas, only the first three of which are included in *Love for Love*. Taylor (*Life of Congreve*, pp. 77–79) questions Congreve's authorship of the ballad. The matter is discussed further by the present writer, "The Ballad in Congreve's *Love for Love*," in *PMLA*, XLVIII (1933), 953–954; and by A. E. H. Swaen, "The Authorship of 'A Soldier and a Sailor'," *Archiv*, CLXVIII (1935), 237–240.

He gave me a Tatler he had written out as blind as he is, for little Harrison. 'Tis about a scoundrel that was grown rich and went out and bought a *coat of arms* at the Herald's, and a set of ancestors at Fleet-ditch; 'tis well enough, and shall be printed in two or three days and if you read those kind of things, this will divert you.

Congreve joined Swift in exposing the fraudulent almanac maker, John Partridge. This drunken cobbler, turned astrologer, had moved into London from Brentford, had dropped his baptismal name of Newsom for one made famous by a star gazer in the time of Elizabeth, and had begun to publish his "infallible" prophecies during the reign of Charles II. It is no wonder that he flourished, in an age in which even Dryden cast horoscopes. For twenty years the literary men had made an honest effort to suppress this irrepressible quack. Gullible London was suffering under Partridge very much as it had a hundred years earlier under the rascals exposed by Jonson in his *Alchemist*. Congreve was glad to join with Swift in a hoax which finally put the old astrologer to rout.

Partridge protected his reputation by the ambiguity of his yearly prophecies:

At the beginning of this Month the Sun meets the Square of Saturn, from which you may Expect some damnable intrigue of the Papists, newly Contrived . . . But besides this, it shews the death of some infirm old Statesman, or else he is turned out and discarded. It Likewise gives ground for new differences between great and eminent men, and there shall arise quarrels between those that least expected it. . . . [36]

Swift exposed this quackery by publishing the *Predictions for the Year 1708*, by "Isaac Bickerstaff, Esq." Squire Bickerstaff, an honest astrologer disgusted with the vague prophecies of John Partridge, boldly predicted the exact day on which various great persons would die. Partridge would "infallibly dye upon the 29th of March next, about Eleven at Night, of a raging Fever." On March 30 Swift had in the hands of the London hawkers an elegy on Partridge, and a few days later a most circumstantial account of his death. Partridge's triumphant announcement that he had not died according to the prediction of the rascal Bickerstaff gave Swift a good opportunity for another thrust at Partridge in *The Vindication of Isaac Bickerstaff, Esq.* Swift brought forward a half dozen arguments

---

[36] From *Annus Mirabilis* as quoted by William Alfred Eddy, "The Wits *vs.* John Partridge, Astrologer," *SP*, XXIX (1932), 29–40. For other new information about Partridge by the same author see "Tom Brown and Partridge the Astrologer," *Modern Philology*, XXVIII (1930–31), 163–168.

to prove the old astrologer actually dead. "Mr. Partridge pretends to tell Fortunes," said Swift, "and recover stolen Goods; which all the Parish says, he must do by conversing with the Devil, and other evil Spirits: And no wise Men will ever allow he could converse personally with either, till after he was dead."

Then Congreve joined in the fun. He brought out a pretended defense of Partridge against his tormentors, entitled *'Squire Bickerstaff Detected*. In the essay, Partridge is made to review the "hard Usage I have receiv'd from the virulent Papers and malicious Practices of this pretended Astrologer," Squire Bickerstaff. He tells how he had been disturbed by the tolling of the bell for his funeral and the measurements taken in his house for mourning. Then he continues:

Well, once more I get my Doors clos'd, and prepare for Bed, in hopes of a little Repose after so many ruffling Adventures; just as I was putting out my Light in order to it, another bounces as hard as he can knock; I open the Window, and ask who's there, and what he wants? I am *Ned*, the Sexton, replies he, and come to know whether the Doctor left any Orders for a Funeral Sermon, and where he is to be laid, and whether his Grave is to be Plain or Brickt? Why, Sirrah, says I, you know me well enough, you know I am not dead; and how dare you affront me, after this manner? Alack a day, Sir, replies the Fellow, why, 'tis in Print, and the whole Town knows you are dead; why, there's Mr. *White*, the Joyner, is but fitting Screws to your Coffin, he'll be here with it in an instant, he was affraid you wou'd have wanted it before this Time. Sirrah, Sarrah, says I, you shall know to morrow, to your Cost, that I am alive, and alive like to be. Why, 'tis strange, Sir, says he, you should make such a Secret of your Death, to us that are your Neighbours; it looks as if you had a Design to defraud the Church of its Dues; and let me tell you, for one that has lived so long by the Heavens, that's unhandsomly done. Hist, hist, says another Rogue that stood by him, away Doctor into your Flanel Gear as fast you can, for here's a whole Pack of Dismals coming to you with their black Equipage; and how indecent will it look for you to stand frightning Folks at your Window, when you should have been in your Coffin this Three Hours?

And so Congreve goes on to mention the many indignities that had been heaped upon the old astrologer, even to his being dunned for the expenses of his own funeral. *'Squire Bickerstaff Detected* made the whole town laugh anew at the quackery of Partridge. The Company of Stationers dropped Partridge from its list, thus cancelling his right to the annual publication of his ridiculous almanac. And the courts were so convinced of the necessity for suppressing the old rascal that the Lord Chancellor refused to listen to the plea of Partridge's lawyer.

CHAPTER VIII

AMONG THE KIT-CATS

I

WHEN Congreve was not at home in the Strand, he was frequently to be found at the country seat of a fellow Kit-Cat.

"The Kit-cat Club, generally mentioned as a set of wits, [were] in reality the patriots that saved Britain."[1] When Horace Walpole wrote this, he was thinking of the long, persistent fight made by his distinquished father and other members of the club for the principles of the Revolution of 1688. Throughout the reign of Queen Anne, while the Tory ministry vacillated between the House of Hanover and the Pretender at Saint-Germain, the Kit-Cats thought only of the Protestant succession. The Tory Bolingbroke was secretly planning to bring back the Pretender on the death of the Queen. One of his lieutenants he put in charge of strategic English ports; another he placed over Scotland. The political leaders among the Kit-Cats, all of them staunch Whigs, had for four years been shut out of the government. But as Queen Anne lay dying, the Duke of Somerset, the most august member of the club, entered the Privy Council without summons and made possible the proclamation of George I. Once the populace had begun to shout "Long live King George!" it was too late for a minority to force the Pretender James on the English nation.

If the Kit-Cat Club had been only a political organization, we might dismiss it promptly. But it was also "a set of wits." Even during the period of its greatest political activity, the club enjoyed prestige chiefly for its interest in *belles-lettres*. Before it opened its doors to the great Whig nobles, it was a modest group of young but promising poets meeting weekly with Jacob Tonson. At that time the little group had no name, and yet it was already "an assembly of good fellows, meeting under certain conditions," and thus, according to the Great Lexicographer's own definition, worthy to be called a club.

Although some details in the long history of the Kit-Cat Club may be obscure, on one matter there is entire agreement: Jacob Tonson founded it and dominated it throughout its activity. In its heyday,

[1] *Anecdotes of Painting in England* (London, 1849), II, 591. For a brief history of the Kit-Cat Club and reproductions of the portraits of the forty-eight members with biographical sketches see *Memoirs of the Celebrated Persons Composing the Kit-Cat Club* (London, 1821).

in the summer of 1703, Tonson spent a few months in Amsterdam and
the Kit-Cats discontinued meetings in his absence. On 22 June 1703
the Duke of Somerset wrote to him: "Our club is dissolved till you
revive it again, which we are impatient of."[2] During the following
month Vanbrugh wrote to Tonson: " . . . the Kit Catt too, will never
meet without you, so you see here's a generall Stagnation for want of
you."[3] Further evidence of Tonson's prominence appears in Sir Richard Blackmore's *The Kit-Cats*, published in 1708.

> Do thou, great *Bocai* [Jacob] smooth thy spacious Brow,
> And one kind Smile on my Attempt bestow:
> For thou, whose fertile Genius does abound
> With noble Projects, didst this Order found.
> And still dost cherish, cultivate and guide
> Thy humble Creature and with decent Pride
> Dost, like the *God of Wine*, the *Kit-Cat* state *bestride*.
> Gracious appear, as when thou mount's thy Seat
> High in the great Assembly, to create
> Some Peer a Member of the *Kit-Cat*-State.

Much has been made of the fact that Tonson, a mere tradesman
and the son of a barber-surgeon in Holborn, should have presided
over the most distinguished club of the age, composed largely of
dukes and earls and men of genius. But Tonson was no ordinary bookseller. He was quick to see that the great epic which Milton had sold
for a pittance might be made the basis of a fortune. He purchased,
first, one half of the copyright, and then, when his finances permitted, the whole. He showed his pride in the masterpiece—and his
gratitude for the wealth it had brought him—by sitting for his Kit-
Cat portrait with a large volume of *Paradise Lost* in his right hand.

Tonson must have been a pleasant companion. Pope, who was not
noted for saying many kind things about publishers, called him "genial *Jacob*."[4] Sometimes his shrewdness and his desire to drive a good
bargain angered one or another of the poets. Dryden, extremely irritated, is said to have sent the bookseller a satirical pen picture in
which his likeness is drawn:

> With leering-look, bull-faced, and freckled fair,
> With two left legs, and Judas-coloured hair,
> And frowsy pores, that taint the ambient air.

"Tell the dog," said Dryden to his messenger, "that he who wrote

[2] *Memoirs of the Celebrated Persons Composing the Kit-Cat Club*, p. vi.
[3] *Works*, ed. Dobrée and Webb, IV, 8.
[4] *The Dunciad* (1728), Book I, 1. 45.

these can write more."[5] Tonson showed his astuteness by hastening
to pacify the angry poet.

But with all his geniality and astuteness, Tonson could hardly
have become an intimate of so many great noblemen if he had not
first built around himself a group of such literary distinction that the
nobles felt themselves honored by being admitted. During the reign
of King William, we are told, war was too much in the sovereign's
thoughts to permit any attention to the poets. So Tonson made them
his "tender Care":

> He still caress'd the unregarded Tribe,
> He did to all their various Tasks prescribe;
> From whence to both great Aquisitions came,
> To him the Profit, and to them the Fame.[6]

Once each week he dined the poets: "Their Drink was gen'rous Wine,
and *Kit-Cat's* Pyes their Meat." The members of the group were carefully selected—"Tho' not of Title, Men of Sense and Wit."[6] Ned
Ward, speaking more satirically, calls the early members of the club
"a parcel of poetical young sprigs that had just weaned themselves
of their mother university."[7] But he does add that "every week the
listening town was charmed with some wonderful offspring of their
teeming noddles, and the fame of the Kit-Cat began to extend itself
to the utmost limits of our learned metropolis." Finally their reputation became so great "that many of the quality grew fond of sharing
the everlasting honour that was likely to crown the poetical society."

The period of this rising fame, when many applied to founder Tonson for admission and when "Men of Title did his Leve wait," must
have been near the turn of the century. Congreve had become one of
the group at a much earlier period, when he was, indeed, something
of a "poetical young sprig" fresh from the university. As early as
1693 a close intimacy had grown up between the young dramatist
and his thirty-seven-year-old publisher. When Congreve went away
to Tunbridge Wells in the summer of that year, he looked to Tonson
as a medium for forwarding letters to Ireland and getting his own
parcels sent down from London. His cordial letters written to Tonson
in August, 1693, conclude with "your affectionate friend" or "your
most affectionate friend,"—in striking contrast with the "most obedient humble servant" that ordinarily closes his letters.

Nicholas Rowe has delightfully revealed in an imaginary conver-

---

[5] See *Memoirs of the Famous Persons Composing the Kit-Cat Club*, pp. 236, 237.
[6] See Blackmore's *The Kit-Cats*.
[7] *Secret History of Clubs*, as quoted by the *Memoirs*, pp. 240–245.

sation the intimacy between the two men.[8] Tonson's query,

> While at my House in *Fleet-street* once you lay,
> How merrily, dear Sir, Time pass'd away?

brings from Congreve the hearty response:

> Thou, Jacob Tonson, wert, to my conceiving,
> The chearfullest, best, honest Fellow living.

Congreve was very much at home among the Kit-Cats. To many of the members he was bound by family ties or mutual interests. The Earl of Burlington owned the Irish estates formerly managed by Congreve's father. Other family contacts were with the young Earl of Huntingdon, half-brother of Congreve's cousin, and with Evelyn Pierrepont, Duke of Kingston, whose grandfather had stood sponsor at the baptism of Congreve's father. Most vital of all were the personal intimacies with literary members—Steele, Walsh, Garth, Addison, and Vanbrugh. Among these Congreve was, at the turn of the century, easily the most distinguished, and served as a kind of poet laureate for the principles of the Revolution. He celebrated with odes and ballads the significant events in the reigns of William and Anne. He sang the praises of William as warrior and peacemaker. He glorified the victories of Marlborough and other Kit-Cat leaders.

The Kit-Cats met with Tonson at various places. Some of the early meetings were in Sheer Lane at the shop of Christopher ("Kit") Cat, who made a mutton pie much to the satisfaction of the group. Indeed the name of this pastry cook is said to have suggested the name adopted by the club. When he moved to the Fountain Tavern in the Strand, a little to the west of Somerset House, the group followed him there for their weekly meetings. Sometimes, especially in the summer, the club assembled at the Upper Flask Tavern on Hampstead Heath. Beginning in 1703, when Tonson took a house a few miles up the Thames at Barn Elms, the club frequently met there. As late as 1725 Vanbrugh still remembered "the first Supper in the Kitchen at Barns"[9]—the best meal that he had ever eaten.

Tonson spent the summer of 1703 in Amsterdam on business while his new house was being made ready. In the meantime the Kit-Cats were eager to resume the meetings of their group. Congreve wrote to Tonson and urged his speedy return:

---

[8] Rowe's poem, entitled "The Reconcilement between Jacob Tonson and Mr. Congreve. An Imitation of Horace, Book III, Ode IX," was apparently first published in *The Muses Mercury*, March, 1707. The title suggests more estrangement between the two men than the poem itself.

[9] *Works*, ed. Dobrée and Webb, IV, 167.

Congreve at the Age of Thirty-Eight

London July 1st 1703

Dear Mr Tonson

My having been at the Bathe prevented my receiving your letter so soone as I should have don, had I been in town, & I was in hopes you would have been here before, but by your staying so much longer I hope you will doe your businesse effectually. I shewd your letter to my Lord Halifax & desired [h]im to do you right to Sr Harry Furnes. I hope the weather will continue fair for yr return since it is changed so much for the better. I thank you for the care & trouble you have taken about my linnen I could wish for halfe a dozen a degree coarser if yr. time & leisure permits you. Your nephew told me of Copies that were dispersed of the Pastoral & likely to be printed so we have thought fit to prevent 'em & print it our selves. I believe barn-elms wants you & I long to see it but dont care to satisfie my curiosity before you come. My humble service to Mr. Addison I am

Yrs most faithfull
& affectionately Willm: Congreve[10]

It was already planned that each member of the club should present his picture to Tonson at his new home. To this plan Vanbrugh referred in writing to Tonson on June 15, 1703:

In short, the Kit-Cat wants you, much more than you ever can do them. Those who remain in towne, are in great desire of waiting on you at Barne-Elmes; not that they have finished their pictures neither; tho' to excuse them (as well as myself), Sr Godfrey has been most in fault. The fool has got a country house near Hampton Court, and is so busy about fitting it up (to receive nobody), that there is no getting him to work.

Congreve was one of those not ready with his picture. It was not painted till 1709, and many were finished even later. All told, forty-eight portraits were painted by Sir Godfrey Kneller, himself a Kit-Cat, and were hung in a room specially prepared for them at Barn Elms. This highly ornamented room, twenty feet wide and forty feet long, had walls high enough—eighteen feet—to accommodate the pictures in two rows around the room. Congreve's hung in the lower row, between portraits of Vanbrugh and Addison.

Each portrait, twenty-eight inches by thirty-six inches, was slightly less than a half length but large enough to show one hand. Sir Godfrey was passionately fond of painting hands. He painted his own portrait for the club with hand raised and index finger pointing, in

---

[10] Congreve's original halographic letter to Tonson, dated July 1, 1703, is preserved by the Historical Society of Pennsylvania, Philadelphia. Sir Edmund Gosse, *Life of William Congreve* (London), 1888, p. 154, quoted one sentence from this letter, which was evidently then among the Tonson manuscripts at Bayfordbury, Hertfordshire. The letter is here printed for the first time.

much the same position that he used for Congreve. Since Congreve posed for no other portrait in such an unnatural posture, we may reasonably hold Kneller to blame in this instance. It is hard to believe that any normal person would have chosen to have his picture painted with this affected lift of the hand.

Fourteen years after presenting his portrait at Barn Elms, Congreve had occasion to write Tonson as follows:

Dear Mr. Tonson

My Kinsman Coll Congreve desires by me that you would do him the favour to lend him my picture to have a copy taken of it, I am sure there will be great care taken of it. I am sorry I am not in town now you are to have the pleasure of seeing you. I hope you are well. I am with unalterable esteem & friendship Dear Jacob

Aug 8th

1723

Ever Yrs

Wm Congreve[11]

II

Congreve's party loyalty finally received its reward when his Kit-Cat friends firmly established themselves at the time of the Hanoverian succession. King George I arrived in London in the fall of 1714, and at the end of the year Congreve received, in place of his "little office," a commission as Secretary to the Island of Jamaica. The Whigs were now so firmly entrenched that Congreve had no further cause to fear the loss of office, though his post was subject to the pleasure of the crown. But to make him more secure, his friends obtained, about four years later, a royal patent confirming his appointment "for and during his natural life."[12]

[11] Printed for the first time by kind permission of H. W. Clinton-Baker, Esq., from the original manuscript at Bayfordbury, Hertfordshire.

[12] See Patent Roll No. 3525, 4 George I, Part V, No. 6. A copy of Congreve's commission as Secretary of Jamaica, filling three closely written pages, is preserved in the Original Correspondence of the Board of Trade, C. O. 137, 12, No. 69. This secretaryship was the only lucrative government post ever held by Congreve. On 3 November 1714 he was granted a minor sinecure as one of the five undersearchers of the customs in the port of London (Treasury Out Letters, Customs and Excise, T. 11. 16, p. 167). This position was apparently the one to which Southerne referred as "a Patent place in the Customs of 600 Pds per ann." The Public Records, however, show repeatedly that the salary for an undersearcher of the customs was only £12 annually. The salary is stated very precisely in a special report (T. 42. 2) made by the Commissioners of the Customs entitled "A List of all the Officers Employed in the Customs with the Salaries and Allowances they Respectively receive, distinguishing therein such as are paid out of Incidents from those that are placed upon the Establishment or paid by Dormant Warrant as they stood at Michaelmas 1717." The commissioners received yearly salaries of £1,000, the chief searcher £120, and the undersearchers £12 each. On p. 17 of the report Congreve is listed as one of the undersearchers with a yearly salary of £12 paid by dormant warrant, *with no annual allowance by incidents*. Each

Even if his health had permitted, Congreve would have desired no seat in Parliament, no active place in the government. His ambition did not lead him that way. Since he wanted to be free of business affairs so far as possible, the secretaryship of distant Jamaica was an almost ideal appointment. A special warrant signed by the Secretary of State permitted him to conduct the office by deputy. So long as all went smoothly in Jamaica, Congreve needed to do little more than give his receipt for his share of the yearly fees, which amounted to more than seven hundred pounds. Although this was only a third of the salary enjoyed by Addison as Secretary to Ireland, it was about four times as much as Congreve had ever before received from government office. This made little difference in his frugal way of living, but it made a big change in his financial condition. He now began to build up a little estate by the purchase of South Sea stock[13] and four per cent annuities of the Bank of England.

---

of the undersearchers was allowed a deputy at £60 annually. This difference in salary in favor of the deputy may be explained as a necessary living wage for the man giving his full time to the work, whereas the position as undersearcher was only a minor sinecure. The great difference, however, is remarkable; and it is possible, in spite of the seemingly clear evidence in the Records, that the undersearchers had an income not indicated.

[13] One of Congreve's purchases of stock is recorded in the following note preserved at the Baker Library, Harvard School of Business Administration:

The 14th August 1716

Mr. Grigsby
Sr.
I desire you to let Mr. Moses Beranger accept for me and in my name Two hundred fifty eight pounds South Sea Stock W^{ch}. he will transferr himself

Wm. Congreve

Another note to Mr. Grigsby thirty days later (Harvard Theatre Collection, Widener Library) shows that Congreve then had a total of seven hundred pounds in South Sea Stock:

Surrey Street 13 Sep: 1716

Sr.
Pay to Mr Tho Snow the Dividend on Seven Hundred pounds being all my stock in the South Sea Comp^a. books for two Half years of 3 li pct. each due Mid^r. last and Xmas next this shall be your Sufficient Warrant
To Mr. Grigsby

Wm Congreve

Next spring Congreve sold fifteen hundred pounds of South Sea Stock (see his signed authorization for the transfer, Bodleian MS. 25,427). Congreve's holdings in 1721 are shown by the following note preserved at the Wellesley College Library:

15 Feb. 1721

Sr.
Pray pay my Dividend due at Xmas last past on Two Thousand Five hundred pounds South Sea Stock unto Mr. Thomas Snow whose receipt shall be your discharge
£2500
To Mr. Cha: Lockyer.
at the South Sea House.

Wm Congreve.

Until this time Congreve had been in no condition to make investments. The leanness of his earlier years is evidenced by his diminutive checking account with Messrs Hoare and Company, one of the several goldsmiths keeping "running cashes" in the vicinity of Temple Bar:

1706

Mr. William Congreve Dr	Cr.
Ap 23 To my note ye	Mar 30 By mony reced
30 March......10/15/—	p 2 notes 20G
June 1 To my note ye	& 10G........32/ 5/—
30 March......21/10/—	

1707

July 31 To part of	May 28 By mony reced
ye 28 May.....10/—/—	p. note........30/—/—[14]
Augt 19 To close	
ditto..........20/—/—	

After 1715 Congreve began making sizable transactions through the Bank of England:

> 22 May 1717 To Col Ralph Congreve
>   of Stretton, Staffordshire.....£ 900
> 21 June 1720 To William Nicoll
>   of the Bank of England......£1500
> 25 June 1723 By Joint Stock
>   South Sea Annuities........£1600[15]

[14] From Ledger 7, ff. 169 V, 170 and Ledger 9, ff. 17 V, 18. Other entries, somewhat larger, occur in Ledgers 16 (for 1712) and 25 (for 1723). For permission to examine the original records of Congreve's checking account I am indebted to the courtesy of the officials of Hoare's Bank, 37 Fleet Street, London.

[15] From Folios 1/4478, 139, 3/539. For a statement of Congreve's account with the Bank of England I am greatly indebted to the kindness of W. Marston Acres, Esq., who also furnished copies of the following two letters, both addressed to Humphry Morice, Governor of the Bank of England:

Sr.

I had the favour of y^r. letter yesterday and have no Objection to Mr Maxwells renewall of his authority. besides that your recommendation is of great weight with me. I suppose Mr. Maxwell would be single in the office. I would not do a hard thing by Mr. Wood tho I never see nor hear anything of him. but as he makes no application, I believe he dos not think of it. However, as you were also his security I frankly leave the determination of it to you, & shall in this or any thing in my little power be glad to shew you how much I am with great respect Sr.

Y^r. most
humble & Obedient
servant
Wm Congreve.

Surrey street
Nov^{er}. 2, 1726

At the time of his death Congreve had three thousand pounds in the Bank of England and other securities valued at about seven thousand pounds.

On the whole Congreve's administration of the Jamaica secretary-ship was uneventful. On one occasion, however, the political bicker-ings in the little island were brought home to London. Governor Archibald Hamilton was dominating the Council of Jamaica but was bitterly opposed by the Assembly. Congreve made the mistake of selecting as his deputy Samuel Page, an ardent partisan of the Assembly. The Governor protested the nomination, but found that Congreve, for all his apparent mildness of spirit, would stand firmly behind the man to whom he had promised the office. Congreve won out in the controversy before the Board of Trade, and Page was in-stalled as the Secretary's deputy. After a few months the Governor induced the Council to remove Page on the ground of incompetency. Almost immediately the Assembly came to his defense and brought in a report commending the deputy for his "great exactness" and gen-eral efficiency. The hostility between Governor and Assembly cul-minated the following month in Page's secret departure for London as a representative from the Assembly to lay before the Board of Trade charges that Hamilton was conspiring with the Spaniards. The Governor was arrested and brought to England, where he set about defending himself and also planning revenge on Samuel Page. Soon the Board "ordered that a letter be writ to Mr. Congreve, Sec-retary of Jamaica, acquainting him with their lordships desire to speak with him on Wednesday next, upon several complaints that have been made to them against Mr. Page, his deputy." Congreve replied to the secretary of the Board in the following letter:[16]

Sr

I had the favour of yrs & sent to Mr. Walter who has all along drawn up the writings in this affair, but he is out of town on the Dorsetshire Election. he is expected to return by the beginning of next week & then I will not fail to let you know what day the writing may be executed. I heartily wish you your health and am Sr. with particular respect.   Yr. most Obedient
Surry street.   humble servant
    feb: 7th, 1726/7   Wm. Congreve

[16] The original letter is preserved in the Original Correspondence for Jamaica, C. O. 137. 12, No. 72. For other documents at the P. R. O. bearing on the controversy between the Governor and Congreve's deputy, see C. O. 137. 10, Nos. 77, 79; C. O. 137. 12, No. 67; C. O. 137. 46, fols. 52, 128–140, 143, 146. See also *Journals of the Assembly of Jamaica*, II (Jamaica, 1795), pp. 170, 192, 195; *Journals of the Com-missioners for Trade and Plantations from March 1714/5 to October 1718 Preserved in the Publc Record Office* (London, 1924), pp. 74, 271–278, 299, 343. The controversy is treated from the point of view of the Governor in an anonymous poem entitled *The Politicks and Patriots of Jamaica* (London, 1718).

Ashley October ye 6th. 1717

Sr.

After a Fitt of Illness of two Month's continuance, I am but just gott into ye Country for the recovery of my health, and am altogether unable to wait upon the Lords Comrs. as you signify to me they desire I shou'd doe.

I beg ye favour of you to acquaint them of this from me with all due respects to their Lps.

And if you please you may also intimate to their Lps. that I have already given Satisfaction to both the Principal Secretarys of State in what relates to me concerning Mr. Page. I am,

Sr.

Your most humble servt.

Wm Congreve

Even during his sickness Congreve had not failed to speak in behalf of his deputy. His efforts, however, were of no avail in the face of Hamilton's continued opposition, and a few months later Page was finally dismissed. Congreve next exerted himself to secure for his late deputy the proper income for his services, and submitted to the Privy Council "the humble petition of William Congreve Esqr. Secretary of the Island of Jamaica, on the behalf of himself and Samuel Page."[17] The petition was altogether unnecessary to insure Congreve's personal income from the office: the Governor had been careful to take "such Care that the Interest of Mr. Congreve the Patentee shall in no way suffer." But the Governor had tried to divert from Page some of the income that should have been his as deputy. Congreve's lawyer had won the case for Page in Jamaica, and now Congreve did what he could to prevent any miscarriage in London.

III

As Congreve grew older and lost taste for the bustling life at court and coffeehouse, he turned for his social contacts to a few old and tried friends, chiefly to persons with whom he had been associated in the Kit-Cat Club. He went out to dine with them at their homes or at taverns, and he sat too long over the heavy food and the good wine. While still in his thirties, he had to admit to Keally, "I am grown fat . . . puzzled to buckle my shoe."[18] He continued to struggle against the tendency toward corpulence and was displeased when one

[17] P. R. O., C. O. 137. 12, No. 101. The petition shows that the fees for the office of Secretary of Jamaica from 9 March to 6 August 1716 amounted to £641:5:8. Since the fees were divided equally between the Secretary and the deputy, Congreve's income from the office for a full year was apparently between seven and eight hundred pounds.

[18] Congreve to Keally, 14 October 1704.

painter drew him as somewhat more "chuffy" than his figure justified.

As a means of keeping his weight within bounds and of combating his tendency to gout, Congreve drank the bottled mineral water available at the coffeehouses. His account for "Spaw water" is still preserved in the original ledger kept by Tom Twining at his coffeehouse in Devereux Court, the Strand:[19]

Mr Congreve

1716		C					
Jany	31	142	To 1 flask Spaw water..........£	1	3		
Feby	2	143	To 1 Do......................	1	3		
	4		To 1 Do.....................	1	3		
	5	144	To 1 Do......................	1	3		
	7	146	To 1 Do......................	1	3		
	8		To 1 Do......................	1	3		
	9	147	To 1 Do......................	1	3		
	10	148	To 1 Do......................	1	3		
	10	149	To 1 Do......................	1	3		
	14	150	To 1 Do......................	1	3		
	15		To 1 Do......................	1	3		
	16	151	To 1 Do......................	1	3		
	18	152	To 1 Do......................	1	3		
	20	153	By Cash in full................	16	3	16	3
Mar	15	168	To 3 half ounces Tea...........	2	10½		
1717							
Nov	22	340	By Cash in full			2	10½
1718				19	1½	19	1½
June	20	501	To 1 flask Spaw water..........	1	3		
	25	505	To 1 Do......................	1	3		
		506	By Cash in full................			2	6
				£1 1	7	1 1	7
July	26	534	To 2 flasks Spaw water.........	2	6		
	28	535	To Do........................	2	6		
	31	537	To 14 flasks Do—15 c & hamper .	18	6		
Aug	16	550	To 6 flasks Do.................	7	6		
	25	555	To 6 flasks Do.................	7	6		
	30	560	By Cash in full................			1 18	6
				3 0	1	3 0	1

[19] For permission to copy the original record I am indebted to the kindness of Stephen H. Twining, Esq., of Messrs. R. Twining & Company, Limited, 216 in the Strand, London.

Sept	4	564	To 6 flasks Spaw Water.........		7	6			
	9	568	To 6 flasks Ditto..............		7	6			
	16	3	To 6 Do......................		7	6			
Oct:	25	16	By Cash in full................				1	2	6

£4: 2 7   4: 2 7

Freedom from set duties gave Congreve opportunity to spend part of his summers in easy retirement with his friends and patrons. He must have been a welcome guest at Bushy Park, seat of Lord Halifax, near Hampton Court. One summer, at least, he spent in the country with the Duke of Montagu. To no place, however, did he go with more satisfaction than to Stowe, Buckinghamshire, home of Sir Richard Temple, the "Dear Dick" to whom Congreve addressed one of his translations and to whom he sent two of his poetic letters. After Congreve's death Temple erected in his gardens at Stowe a monument to commemorate the "elegant, polished Wit" of Congreve the dramatist and the "candid, most unaffected Manners" of Congreve his friend.[20]

In the autumn of 1717 Congreve slipped away from London to recuperate from an illness at Ashley, the seat of Richard Boyle, Viscount Shannon, another Kit-Cat friend. Ashley was near Walton-upon-Thames only a few miles beyond Pope's villa in Twickenham. Two years later, Congreve was again at Ashley. He was still in poor health, and his eyes were so weak that he had to appeal to Lord Shannon to write this short letter to Pope:

Ashley thursday [1719]

Sr.

By candle light Mr. Congreve wants a Scribe, he has not been well indeed, but will take the air your way to morrow morning. Don't let this be any restraint on you, for he is not Qualified for long visits. Since you were so kind to mention me in your letter, I hope you'l keep your promiss, and let me have the pleasure of seeing you here what day is most Convenient for you next weeke, and it will be a very great satisfaction to S[r].

Yo[r] most humble
Se[t]
Shannon[21]

Congreve's eyes had been troubling him for years. On 26 October 1710 Swift found Congreve at his lodgings in Surrey Street nearly blind with cataracts which could be removed only after several years

---

[20] See *A Description of the Gardens of Lord Viscount Cobham, at Stowe in Buckinghamshire.* The Fifth Edition, corrected and enlarg'd (Northampton, 1748), pp. 25, 26.

[21] This letter, called to my attention by the kindness of Professor George Sherburn, is from the original in the B. M. Homer MSS. Add. 4808, f. 172.

of waiting. During 1712 he was under the treatment of a French ocu-
list,[22] and perhaps the cataracts were removed at that time. His eyes
continued to cause trouble for a number of years, if not till the end of
his life. But Congreve did not become blind, as some have supposed.
Many documents written in his own hand have been preserved for
the period from 1710 till 1727; and it should be added that letters
written in 1726 and 1727 indicate that Congreve's vision was then
clearer than it had been ten years earlier.

However blind and gouty Congreve became, he did not let his
physical condition sour his spirits. In 1710 Swift was amazed to find
him, in the midst of his afflictions, "as cheerful as ever." Swift returned again and again to sit for hours with Congreve and afterwards
to report to Stella that he had been "to see Will. Congreve, who is a
very agreeable companion."[23] In 1723 Gay wrote Swift that Congreve
was still laboring "under the same afflictions, as to his sight and gout"
but had "not lost anything of his cheerful temper."[24] These reports
are in keeping with the story that when Congreve lay on his death
bed he was worried lest anyone be inconvenienced. Congreve had certain rare qualities which made him, invalid though he was, a welcome
visitor at Ashley and other country seats of the Kit-Cats.

After returning to London from Ashley in the fall of 1719, Congreve was asked by a fellow Kit-Cat, the young Duke of Newcastle,
to pass judgment upon Thomas Southerne's tragedy, *The Spartan
Dame*. As Lord Chamberlain, entrusted with the censorship of the
stage, the Duke wished to know whether the production of Southerne's play, which had been banned from the stage many years before
because of some supposed political implications, could now be safely
permitted. He turned to Congreve as a good critic and safe party
man. No doubt Congreve was glad to have an opportunity to repay
the kindness of Southerne nearly thirty years before in helping with
the staging of *The Old Bachelor*. On Congreve's recommmendation[25]
the Lord Chamberlain authorized the performance of *The Spartan
Dame*, and Southerne is said to have realized from the play the neat
sum of five hundred pounds.

IV

There was something disarming about Congreve's frankness and
honesty, something contagious about his generosity. He had the art

---

[22] See Swift's *Journal to Stella*, 5 January 1711/2, and Congreve to Keally, 6 May 1712.
[23] *Journal to Stella*, 26 October 1710 and 8 July 1711.
[24] See Swift's *Correspondence*, ed. F. Elrington Ball, 3 February 1722/3.
[25] See Congreve's undated letter to the Duke of Newcastle, in the edition by
Dobrée, p. 521.

of getting along with people. Crusty old John Dennis quarreled with almost everybody, but not with Congreve. At one time Congreve was even able to bring about a truce between Dennis and his bitterest enemy, Pope. For Congreve, Pope had a deep and sincere friendship that had begun many years before, when Pope, a youngster in his 'teens, timidly brought out his pastorals. Congreve had been one of the first to commend them to Tonson, and Pope never forgot that Congreve had "loved" his early poems. When Pope was getting subscriptions for his *Iliad*, he knew that the list of subscribers was being materially increased by Congreve's quiet, persistent influence among his many titled friends. Pope was duly appreciative. He expressed that appreciation in a fine way by dedicating to Congreve the translation of the *Iliad*.

Pope's decision to inscribe his work to Congreve was not made hastily as the final volume was going to press. Pope had made up his mind at least as early as 1719, when he jotted down in his manuscript: "End the notes with a dedication to Mr. Congreve, as a memorial of our friendship occasioned by his translation of this last part of Homer." He also made a point of incorporating two of Congreve's lines in his translation and of calling attention to them in a note.

As soon as the first volume of the *Iliad* was ready for publication, Pope made sure that Congreve received his copy well in advance of the regular subscribers. The *Post Boy* for Tuesday, 31 May 1715, announced that "the Subscribers for Mr. Pope's Translation of Homer" might get the first volume "on Monday the 6th Day of June next" from the publisher Bernard Lintott. Congreve's holographic receipt for his copy, five days in advance, is still preserved:

> June 1st 1715
> Received of Mr. Lintott the first volume
> of Mr. Popes translation of Homer
> by me Wm Congreve[26]

Jealous and suspicious though Pope often was, he never doubted Congreve. Except for Swift and Gay, Congreve was perhaps Pope's most intimate literary friend. After Congreve's death Pope made, in his list of departed friends, this note for Congreve: "*poeta, eximius, vir comis, urbanus, et mihi perquam familiaris.*" "Exceedingly intimate with me"—he could hardly have been more emphatic. It is no wonder that in writing to the Earl of Oxford, Pope should stress his "long twenty years' friendship" with Congreve and say feelingly of his death, "It . . . struck me through."[27]

---

[26] From the Huntington Library.   [27] See the letter dated 21 January 1728/29.

Congreve's amiable disposition kept him almost free from legal en-
tanglements. He never took a case to law. Once, however, in his last
years he was unwillingly involved in a suit that irked him exceedingly. It was the famous suit begun as early as 1698 by the Duke of
Hamilton to secure certain moneys which he considered due from the
estate of his late father-in-law, Lord Gerrard. The long-continued
case led to the fatal duel between the Duke and the notorious Lord
Mohun. Lady Mohun, against whom the Duchess of Hamilton now
brought suit, managed by various legal devices to postpone the decision from year to year. Before her death in June, 1725, she executed
a deed of limitation, putting all her possessions in the hands of the
Duke of Argyle, the Earl of Ilay, William Congreve, Moses Beranger,
Charles Mordaunt, or any one of these. Congreve found himself de-
fendant in a case involving fifteen thousand pounds. Nine months
later, on 14 May 1726, he filed "The severall answer of William Congreve Esquire . . . to the Bill of Complaint of the most noble Elizabeth Duchess of Hamilton," in which he swore that he was "an
absolute stranger" to the whole affair, that he had been appointed
trustee without his knowledge or consent, that he had never acted as
trustee or possessed himself of any part of the estate. Finally, he
prayed the court that he be "dismissed with his reasonable costs and
charges."[28] And thus ended Congreve's first and last day in court.

In the same year the aging Congreve had another experience that
disturbed his well-loved ease and quiet as much as the suit in chancery. Congreve had consistently avoided the attentions of his ad-
mirers. In the first flush of his reputation as a writer he had slipped
into and out of town to get away from publicity. As he grew older this
hero-worship harassed him. He preferred to stay away from court and
coffeehouse. He did not consider it modest to talk of his "great" plays,
the plays that he had written a quarter of a century before. All his
life he had spoken of them as "poor trifles" or "homely fare."[29] So
when the brilliant young Frenchman, Voltaire, heaped profuse flat-
tery upon the old dramatist, he was genuinely embarrassed. Illnesses
and the daily struggles of life had in some measure sapped Congreve's
urbanity, and he may have sounded curt when he asked to be visited
"upon no other Foot than that of a Gentleman, who led a Life of
Plainness and Simplicity." Voltaire, not knowing his man, chose to
mistake genuine humility for snobbery and said openly that he "was

[28] For the suit of the Duchess of Hamilton against Congreve see P. R. O., Chancery
Proceedings, 1714–58, Bundle 2172, No. 19, and Bundle 2221, No. 53. Congreve's
answer to the suit is attached to Bundle 2221, No. 53.

[29] See the prefaces and dedications to his plays and his letter to Giles Jacob.

very much disgusted at so unseasonable a Piece of Vanity."[30] No
other contemporary pronounced Congreve vain. To Dryden, Pope,
Swift, Steele, Gay, and others most closely associated with him, Congreve was known for his "modesty," his "sweetness" of temper, his
"Aequanimity, candour and Benevolence," his humility "in the
height of envy'd honors," his helpfulness, his frankness and sincer-
ity.[31] But posterity was to be perverse enough to ignore the unani-
mous estimate of those who lived with Congreve and knew him best,
and to accept as final the impression of a passing foreigner.

---

[30] *Letters Concerning the English Nation*, Number XIX, as reprinted with introduction by Charles Whibley (London, 1926).

[31] See, for example, Dryden's lines "To My Dear Friend Mr. Congreve"; Steele's
lines "To Mr. Congreve, Occasion'd by his Comedy Call'd *The Way of the World*,"
and his Dedication to Addison's *The Drummer*, London, 1722; "A Poem to the
Memory of Mr. Congreve," London, 1729; Gay's poem entitled "Mr. Pope's Welcome
from Greece"; the *Gentleman's Magazine*, IX (1738), 20, 21; and the references to
Congreve in the correspondence of Swift, Pope, Dryden, and Gay.

CHAPTER IX

THE YOUNG DUCHESS OF MARLBOROUGH

I

THE passing years finally brought to Congreve a love that completely filled his life. The town gossiped about the inseparable companionship between him and Henrietta, Duchess of Marlborough. Even when death had separated them rumors persisted that were none too kind to this great lady. Over the tea tables people snickered at a reference in *The Daily Post* to "the Effigies of the late ingenious William Congreve, Esq; done in Waxwork" and "kept at a Person of Quality's House in St. James's."[1] Yes—so they gabbled—

[1] In *The Daily Post* for Saturday, 15 July 1732, appeared the following notice: "We hear that the Effigies of the late ingenious William Congreve, Esq; done in Waxwork, at the Expense of 200 l. and which was kept at a Person of Quality's House in St. James's, was broke to Pieces by the Carelessness of a Servant in bringing it down Stairs last Monday Night." This paragraph was the inspiration the following year for a scurrilous poem, *The Amorous D[uc]h[e]ss: or, Her G[race] Grateful*. The poem tells how "Great Hotonto" (Henrietta, Duchess of Marlborough) had erected a tomb for "Comick Con" (Congreve) and also had provided for herself "*Pictures* and *Prints*" of "ingenious Conny." But wanting "something more of Substance," she had called in an artist and had directed him how

> To raise in Wax the GOD-LIKE man. . . .
> The Figure form'd, with lively Grace,
> Having for *Niche, a curious Case*,
> She visits oft the *dear-lov'd* Place.
> Breaths out her soft desires, some say,
> Full half a Dozen Times a Day;
> And thus, for Years, she had gone on,
> As if she never meant t' have done
> Lamenting for Appollo's Son.

The second canto of the poem tells how the servant Tom, in carrying the statue from one room to another, drops it and breaks it into many pieces. Hotonto is in wild despair. She rends her hair, she fasts, she groans. She orders Tom summarily dismissed, refusing to see "Her Conny's *Murderer*." Then she calls on "Connelia" (her young daughter Mary) to help her pick up the sacred fragments from the floor:

> Come, dear Connelia, come my Love,
> Help me the *Manes* to remove.
> Let 'em no longer on the floor
> Be strew'd about, or trampled o'er;
> Let us collect them, and bemoan;
> For thou must give me Groan for Groan.

London readers of the poem in 1733, four years after Congreve's death, could have had no difficulty in catching the intended relationship between "Conny" and "Con-

his last and enduring love worshiped him, set him up in wax, and ca-
ressed the idol. The second Duchess of Marlborough could hardly have
been fool enough for that. It was scandal, of course—palpably a
falsehood—and yet it represented something of underlying truth. It
spoke of immense devotion. When Congreve died, this Duchess Henrietta did stay by his body all through the night.

We know less about the "young" Duchess Henrietta than we do
of her indomitable mother, the "old" Duchess Sarah. Like her mother
she was a blonde, probably with blue eyes, and with the look that
sits well in miniatures. Her tapering forearms and her slender fingers
were the sort that Kneller loved to paint. In Henrietta the hot-
headedness of the mother was restrained somewhat by "that sweetness of Temper" which distinguished her father. But back of her high
forehead she had a will no less determined than that of her mother.
She refused to allow herself to be dominated by the old Duchess. In
spite of Mother Sarah she continued her enjoyment of country
dances, her ambition "to be a Wit," her generosity to men of letters.
"She has starts," complained old Sarah bitterly, "of giving 100 guineas to a very low poet [John Gay] that will tell her that she is what
she knows she is not, which I think so great a weakness that I had
rather give money not to have such verses made publick."[2]

Henrietta was not a paragon. We may, however, definitely think
of her as good to look upon, and vain, and sweet and charitable, and
very kind to Congreve. We should remember, too, that he who found
so many things to satirize in the ladies of the Restoration found things
in her to love, that he liked to feel her presence about him in the

---

nelia," nor would they miss the significance of the last line, "For thou must give me
Groan for Groan."

The notice in *The Daily Post* makes it clear that Henrietta did have a waxen image
of Congreve. The anonymous author of *The Amorous D[uc]h[e]ss* shows how gossips
could imagine her worshiping at the shrine of her lover. In 1753, twenty years after
the death of Henrietta, Theophilus Cibber's *Lives of the Poets* (IV, 92) reported: "It
is said of Mr. Congreve, that he was a particular favorite of the ladies . . . sprightly
as well as eloquent in his manner, and so much a favorite of Henrietta duchess of
Marlborough, that even after his death, she caused an image of him to be every day
placed at her toilet-table, to which she would talk as to the living Mr. Congreve,
with all the freedom of the most polite and unreserved conversation."

Before the end of the century the image had become (Thomas Davies, *Dramatic
Miscellanies*, 1784, III, 382) an ivory automaton "which was supposed to bow to her
grace and to nod in approbation of what she spoke to it," or (*Biographia Britannica*,
1789, IV, 79) a waxen figure to be served with a variety of foods and attended by
physicians. It remained for Macaulay (*Edinburgh Rev.*, January, 1841), at the middle
of the next century, to provide the Duchess with *two* images—one of ivory and one
of wax.   [2] See Mrs. Arthur Colville, *Duchess Sarah* (New York, 1904), p. 312.

Her Grace, the Dutchess of Marlborough.

HENRIETTA, DUCHESS OF MARLBOROUGH
(1681–1733)

little lodge in Windsor Park or in the drawing rooms of St. James's.

Henrietta was the oldest daughter of John Churchill, Duke of Marlborough, and so she was old enough to marry even before the Duke fought Blenheim. If she could have married afterwards, there is no telling how far up in the peerage she might have married. But as it was, she married Francis Godolphin. That was in the spring of 1698, when Henrietta was not yet eighteen. Whatever love she had for her husband did not last many years. He did not compel affection like his great father, Sidney Godolphin. Francis was kind and patient and long-suffering. Perhaps Chesterfield was unjust in saying that Francis was insignificant, that he went to the House of Lords to sleep and that it mattered little whether he slept on the right or on the left of the Woolsack. But certain it is that he did not have the brilliance and esprit that was Henrietta's delight.

In 1703 fate took a hand. Henrietta's only brother died at Cambridge. He was a likely lad of seventeen, heir to all the Marlborough wealth and titles. Congreve joined the general lament, promptly composed a pastoral, and sent manuscript copies "privately to Condole" the members of the family. Somehow it seemed fitting that death should have brought Henrietta and Congreve together, for she was to know Congreve, not in the freshness of youth, but in a time when he was fighting his way through the shadows of ill health—of gout, and finally of near blindness. Congreve dedicated his poem to Henrietta's father-in-law, the Earl of Godolphin. At that very time Henrietta and Francis were living with the Earl at Godolphin House adjoining St. James's Palace. There Sidney Godolphin died in 1712 and Henrietta became Countess of Godolphin. She never became mistress of the finer Marlborough House, which the Duke, her father, had built in 1709. When the great Duke died in 1722, Henrietta did become Duchess in her own right by special grant of Parliament, and she inherited the bulk of the family wealth, but the old Duchess Sarah had a life interest in Marlborough House and in Blenheim Palace and clung tenaciously to that life for years after Henrietta died in 1733.

But let us return to 1703, when Henrietta was twenty-two years old and Congreve thirty-three. It was in this year, we must remember, that the Earl of Scarsdale made a bequest to Anne Bracegirdle, with the stipulation that it should be "the first Money paid." And it was probably in this year also that Congreve addressed to Anne Bracegirdle the verses, "False tho you've been to me and Love." Three years later, in 1706, Congreve strengthened his attachment to Godolphin House by a second poem, an ode addressed to Sidney

Godolphin, in which he linked Henrietta's father and her father-in-law as England's greatest benefactors:

> Thus, thou Godolphin, dost with Marlbro strive,
> From whose joint Toils we Rest derive:
> Triumph in Wars abroad his Arm assures,
> Sweet Peace at Home thy Care secures.

Henrietta was duly impressed and flattered by the odes sent to Godolphin House by the distinguished poet and dramatist. For her own part, she had "a great mind" to be numbered among the wits. She was marvelously pleased to find, in the prologue with which Vanbrugh and Congreve opened their new theatre in the Haymarket, that she, Henrietta Godolphin, was referred to as "the learn'd Minerva."[3] Before long Congreve was one of those who played cards at Godolphin House. There old Sarah came upon Henrietta and Congreve amid the aces and jacks of ombre and sensed at once that she was a very unwelcome visitor. "He look'd out of Countenance," she later complained to Henrietta, "but Shew'd more willingness to talk to me than You did; I soon put You at ease, by going away."[4]

II

As a very young man Congreve was attracted by women older than he. But time has a way of striking a balance. After the turn of the century, when he was rapidly passing into middle age, his fancy turned to women much younger. One of these was Lady Mary Wortley Montagu, who was baptized in Covent Garden in the very year that brought Congreve to London, a nineteen-year-old boy fresh from college. He was destined to see much of Lady Mary. For generations her family had been friends of the Congreves. Her father, Evelyn Pierrepont, later duke of Kingston, was Congreve's fellow member in the Kit-Cat Club. And there, according to tradition, Lady Mary was introduced by her father when she was only eight years old. Ever afterwards she was to have a kindly feeling for the wits, especially for Congreve. "I never knew anybody," declared Lady Mary, "that had so much wit as Congreve."[5]

[3] See *The History of the English Stage—By Thomas Betterton.* Revised, with additional notes, by Charles L. Coles (Boston, 1814), p. 105.

[4] Our knowledge of Henrietta has been greatly increased by a recent study of Miss Kathleen M. Lynch, "Henrietta, Duchess of Marlborough," *PMLA*, LII (1937), 1072–1093. For Henrietta's desire to be a wit and for Sarah's comment to Henrietta about her actions when found playing cards with Congreve, see a manuscript of the "old" Duchess preserved at Blenheim, *An account of the Dutches of marl. & montagus behaviour before & after their fathers death,* as quoted by Miss Lynch, p. 1083.

[5] Joseph Spence, *Anecdotes,* ed. S. W. Singer (London, 1820), p. 232.

After Lady Mary grew to womanhood, married Wortley Montagu, and went away with him to the embassy at Constantinople, she kept up a warm correspondence with Congreve. Pope, also her correspondent, reported of himself and Congreve: "We never meet but we lament over you: we pay a kind of weekly rites to your memory, where we strow flowers of rhetoric, and offer such libations to your name as it were a profaneness to call toasting."[6]

Both Pope and Congreve wrote to Lady Mary with the usual gallantry, and she replied that she was "warmly sensible" and wished to live in their remembrance, "though dead to all the world beside."[7] Pope became extravagant. Perhaps he worked himself up to a passionate regard for her and was disappointed when he found there was no return. Congreve, whose real interest was in Henrietta, was only playing the gallant. No doubt he did esteem those bright eyes that were down in Turkey noting vaccination for the smallpox. But he must have felt a little warm about the temples if ever he read the poem entitled *The Lover*, in which Lady Mary wrote, "Take, Congreve, at once the inside of my breast." Then she went on to picture her ideal lover:[8]

> No pedant, yet learned; no rake-helly gay,
> Or laughing, because he has nothing to say;
> To all my whole sex obliging and free,
> Yet never be fond of any but me;
> In public preserve the decorum that's just,
> And show in his eyes he is true to his trust.

To such a lover, Lady Mary declared, she would not be "as cold as a virgin in lead." Indeed,

> . . . when the long hours of public are past,
> And we meet with Champagne and a chicken at last,
> May every fond pleasure that moment endear;
> Be banish'd afar both discretion and fear!
> Forgetting or scorning the airs of the crowd,
> He may cease to be formal, and I to be proud,
> 'Till lost in the joy, we confess that we live,
> And he may be rude, and yet I may forgive.

But when Lady Mary returned from Constantinople at the end of 1718, she found that Congreve was devoting himself more and more

---

[6] Pope to Lady Mary, 20 August 1716.

[7] Lady Mary to Pope, 17 June 1717.

[8] See the poem entitled "The Lover" in Lady Mary's *Works*, London, 1803, V, 213–216.

to Henrietta, almost to the point of losing his wonted gallantry. No longer did he appear to be unreservedly "obliging and free" to the whole sex. A few years later even Pope was led to protest in a letter to John Gay: "Pray put Mr. Congreve in mind that he has one on this side of the world who loves him; and that there are more men and women in the universe than Mr. Gay and my Lady Duchess of M[arlborough]. There are ladies in and about Richmond that pretend to value him."[9]

One of these ladies was the brillant Lady Mary, and she was one who could hardly be expected to accept the situation with a very good grace. Ever since she had been toasted as a child by the Kit-Cats, she had been a favorite among the men. It was hard to find herself, like Mrs. Marwood in *The Way of the World*, in competition for a Mirabell who gave all his attention to Millamant.

As for Henrietta, she knew her powers and gloried in her conquest no less than did Millamant:

> 'Tis not to wound a wanton Boy
> Or am'rous Youth, that gives the Joy;
> But 'tis the Glory to have pierc'd a Swain,
> For whom inferior Beauties sigh'd in vain.
>
> Then I alone the Conquest prize,
> When I insult a Rival's Eyes:
> If there's Delight in Love, 'tis when I see
> The Heart which others bleed for, bleed for me.
>   (Act III, Sc. xii.)

Is there not something of Millamant's taunting in this note from Duchess Henrietta to Lady Mary?

I am sure you won't dislike to have Mr. Congreve to-morrow if you can get him, for he is like all good things, hard to come at, and tho' I shan't add to your company, I have wit enough not to spoyle it, which you must allow as being tolerable. What hour would you have me come?[10]

"Hard to come at!" Not for Henrietta. All the world knew how particular Congreve was on her account, to the sad neglect of "inferior Beauties."

At this time London was torn between allegiance to German or Italian music as exemplified by the composers Handel and Bononcini. The Duchess sponsored Bononcini and arranged a series of concerts for the entertainment of the town—and of Congreve, who was pas-

---

[9] 11 September 1722.

[10] As quoted from the unpublished manuscript by Emily Morse Symonds, *Lady Mary Wortley Montagu and Her Times* (London, 1907), p. 310.

sionately fond of music. Lady Mary noted that, though the concerts were frequent, she and the Duchess were "not in that degree of friendship to have *me* often invited." On the surface they remained friends. As Lady Mary expressed it, "We continue to see one another like two people who are resolved to hate with civility."[11]

III

Intent upon Henrietta, Congreve gave increasingly little thought to Lady Mary. Indeed he would spend weeks at Ashley Park near Lady Mary in Twickenham without troubling to call on her, and she naturally felt aggrieved. But for the most part Congreve did not find himself in Lady Mary's vicinity. He was more frequently at Godolphin House in St. James's, at Henrietta's little lodge in Windsor Park, or at one of the fashionable watering places, in search of relief from his ever-recurring gout. Perhaps, like so many, Congreve, instead of finding at Tunbridge Wells a cure, only lost his heart. The middle-aged poet became more and more enamoured with the lady who had "a great mind to be thought a Wit." And the husband? No doubt he was far away in London, safely asleep on the left of the Woolsack.

In later years Congreve turned more to Bath. Thirty-eight hours along the highway toward Bristol brought Londoners to those celebrated hot springs, reputedly discovered by the mythical King Bladud, and certainly used since early Roman days. New glories came to Bath as Queen Anne opened her reign with successive visits to the town. Even more significant for Bath was the arrival about the same time, in 1705, of a penniless fop and adventurer named Richard Nash. Before many years this natural-born Master of Ceremonies, or "King" of Bath, was having his yearly arrival announced by the glorious chime of bells.[12]

The Kingdom of Beau Nash was symbolized by the figure of the Beau standing in the midst of the Assembly Room in gold-laced clothes so fine "that he was taken by many at a distance for a gold garland." He was the idol of the ladies. Even the formidable old Sarah, Duchess of Marlborough, was pleased to receive his visits. No king dominated his realm more completely. He could with impunity snatch the tabooed apron from the Duchess of Queensbury, or deny an extra dance beyond the closing hour of eleven even to the Royal Princess herself. But for all his presumption and his foppishness, King Nash brought order and politeness to Bath and made the little

11 Letters and Works, ed. Lord Wharncliffe (London, 1861), I, 483, 484.

12 For the activities of Beau Nash at Bath see A. Barbeau, *Life & Letters at Bath in the XVIIIth Century* (London, 1904), pp. 22 ff.

city a haven for thousands who came to drink its medicinal waters, to steam themselves in its hot baths, or merely to spend a summer of pleasure.

In 1722, when this watery kingdom was in its golden age, William Congreve spent the whole season at Bath. Another personage then at Bath was Henrietta. In September, as the season was drawing to a close, Pope was lamenting that Congreve had forgotten the existence of any other woman save the Duchess of Marlborough.

By this time the "young" Duchess Henrietta had two grown children. Her son William, Marquis of Blandford, was in his twenty-fourth year, and her daughter Henrietta had already been married five years to the Duke of Newcastle. Two other children born to Henrietta and Francis Godolphin near the turn of the century had died young. For nearly twenty years Henrietta Godolphin had borne no children. But she was still in the vigor of her womanhood, only forty-one years of age, and the waters of Bath were famed for curing barrenness. The traveler John Macky, visiting Bath at this period, noted that the reputation of the place had been enhanced during the preceding century by the experience of King James's Queen Mary, who had bathed in "the *Cross Bath*, which is used by the People of the first Quality," and had given birth the following year to a son. ("These Waters," says Macky, "have a wonderful Influence on barren Ladies, who often prove with Child even in their Husbands Absence.")[13]

John Macky, then, should not have been greatly surprised next year, 1723, when the London newspapers announced that Henrietta, Duchess of Marlborough, had given birth to a daughter. Nor was Lady Mary Wortley Montagu. In fact, she was ready to say some very hard things about "my poor friend the young Duchess of Marlborough," who had "exposed herself to most violent ridicule."[14] Some other things that Lady Mary adds are hardly quotable. No doubt old Sarah, too, spoke her mind, and we may be sure that she had few kind words for her oldest daughter. She is said to have referred to Henrietta regularly as "Congreve's Moll." Later when death had put an end to the affair, she tersely remarked, "I know not what 'pleasure' she might have had in his company, but I am sure it was no 'honour.' "[15]

As for Congreve, he was—like Mirabell—discreet, and there is no reason to believe that he said anything. We have no record that he

[13] *A Journey through England* (London, 1724), II, 121–123.
[14] *Letters and Works*, I, 472.
[15] See Mrs. Arthur Colville, *Duchess Sarah*, pp. 311, 312.

let the gossips worry him. But he did take a significant action in which Henrietta's young daughter Mary was concerned. His will two years after her birth made provisions through which the young girl was destined to inherit his estate.

The phrase "destined to inherit" is used advisedly, for Congreve did not will his property directly to Mary. To do so would have stirred up infinitely more gossip than was already in the air. The end desired could be attained, and much more discreetly, by another method. He could leave his property to the Duchess with the understanding that she would pass it along to the one in whom he was so deeply and so naturally interested.

IV

Congreve's will has continued to puzzle and annoy people even to this day. Why, they ask, should Congreve leave his estate to the Duchess of Marlborough, who was already the wealthiest woman in England? Dr. Johnson declared the answer "either not known or not mentioned," and suggested that the property might better have been left to his ancient family, which was then "reduced to difficulties and distress."[16] The poet Edward Young remarked, "How much better would it have been to have given it to poor Mrs. Bracegirdle."[17] Macaulay saw in the will only more evidence of Congreve's pride and worldliness.[18] Biographers have been frankly mystified and have concluded that "we can know nothing whatever about it."

Lest we should have too much concern over Congreve's failure to provide for his distressed family or for "poor Mrs. Bracegirdle," it should be said at once that neither was suffering. We have already seen that Mrs. Bracegirdle was in easy circumstances. The two hundred pounds that Congreve set aside for her in his will was neither needed to relieve her want nor intended to do so. It was only a pleasant reminder that he had remained her friend, notwithstanding her defection, and that he was "Gratefull for the past."

As for the Congreve family in Staffordshire, it was not in the dire straits suggested by Johnson. Several years after the poet's death the family did sell a part of the estate to satisfy certain obligations. The money realized from that sale, over and above the amount required for debts, was nearly equivalent to the poet's whole estate, and the family still had its original holdings at "Congreve."[19] The poet, then,

[16] *Lives of the English Poets*, ed. G. B. Hill (Oxford, 1905), II, 227.

[17] Dr. Young, quoted by Joseph Spence, *Anecdotes*, ed. Singer (London, 1820), p. 376.

[18] See Macaulay's article in the *Edinburgh Review*, January, 1841.

[19] See the Congreve papers at the William Salt Library, Stafford.

could hardly have considered the family in real need. He had little occasion to fell any obligation, for he had received nothing directly from the estate, and his father had been left only one hundred pounds. This sum the poet returned more than fivefold in small bequests, amounting to five hundred and forty pounds, to his cousins Congreve.

Later events make it all but impossible to escape the inference that Congreve earnestly desired to transfer the bulk of his estate to Henrietta's young daughter Mary. Certain it is that the Duchess, to whom Congreve willed his property, carefully provided in *her* will for the transfer of all his possessions—notably and specifically "all Mr. Congreves Personal Estate"—to her daughter Mary and to Mary's descendants. That Henrietta, in so providing for Mary, was effecting Congreve's wishes seems as certain as the fact that he had carefully arranged to make this possible without scandal or embarrassment. The circumstances, as I see them, were as follows.

First, to return to the will, it is clear enough that no child of the Duchess of Marlborough would need Congreve's little property. But this apparently did not lessen Congreve's desire to have Mary inherit what he had accumulated in bonds, and books, and monogrammed silver. To determine *where* he wished to leave his property was easy. To determine *how* he might accomplish his desire without injury to the woman he loved was difficult indeed. But Congreve was no bungler. He was a careful worker, whether constructing one of those exquisite situations for *The Way of the World* or extricating himself from a delicate situation of his own. And he managed the whole so astutely that for more than two hundred years the true purpose of his will was to remain hidden.

Congreve was so disturbed by the problem before him that he wrote no less than five separate documents—a will and four codicils.[20] Of these we have a record, but we can never know how many other plans he may have made and destroyed. In none of his plans, perhaps, was he rash enough to consider seriously the naming of Mary directly as his heir. The preserved papers indicate that at first Congreve made over his estate to Henrietta and named her as absolute and sole executrix. One of the documents reads:

[20] Congreve's will is not to be found at Somerset House, though several documents preserved there purport to be copies of Congreve's wills and codicils. The originals were taken on 21 February 1728/29 for the use of the executor, Francis, Earl of Godolphin, and a receipt left for a will and four codicils. One of the copies at Somerset House speaks of Henrietta, Duchess of Marlborough, as "sole executrix as is specified in the said will." This must show Congreve's earlier plan, since the will actually probated made Francis executor.

I do hereby confirm, and do hereby revoke and annul all other Legacies therein mentioned, or in the Counter-part of the said Will more at large set down; which Counter-part is by me left in Custody of her Grace, *Henrietta*, Dutchess of *Marlborough*, my sole Executrix, as is specified in the said Will and Counter-part thereof.

As Congreve's sole executrix, Henrietta would clearly be able to transfer his property according to his wishes. But could not the same end be achieved more discreetly? On second thought, Congreve brought in the husband—the patient, long-suffering Francis—and named him as executor: "And in Confidence of the Honesty and Justice of him the said *Francis* Earl of Godolphin, I do hereby constitute and appoint him the sole Executor of this my Will."

What move could more effectively silence the wagging tongues? All the town would know that Francis, Earl of Godolphin, was administrator for Congreve's estate. What it need not know was that the will was drawn in such a way that the administrator would have no check whatever on Henrietta and that she could manage everything just as independently as if she herself had been named sole executrix. Note how carefully Congreve has worded his will:

All the Rest and Residue of my Estate, the same consisting in personal Things only, (not having any Lands, or other real Estate) I give and bequeath to the Dutchess of *Marlborough*, the now Wife of *Francis* Earl of *Godolphin*, in the County of *Cornwall;* but not so as to vest in him the said Earl of *Godolphin*, the equitable Right and Interest of such Rest and Residue, but that the same and every part thereof; and the Interest, Produce, and Benefit thereof; shall and may at all times, from and after my Decease, be had and received by her the said Dutchess, namely, *Henrietta*, Dutchess of *Marlborough*, to her sole and separate Use, and wherewith her said Husband, or any after-taken Husband, of her the said Dutchess of *Marlborough*, shall not intermeddle, or have any controuling Power over: nor shall the said Rest and Residue, or the Interest and Produce thereof, be liable to the Debts and Incumbrances of the said Earl of *Godolphin*, or of any after-taken Husband, of her the said Dutchess of *Marlborough*, in any wise; but shall be had and received, issued and paid, as she the said Dutchess of *Marlborough*, shall by writing under her Hand, from time to time direct and appoint; and her own Acquittance shall be a sufficient Discharge for all, or any Part of the Estate so given to her as afforesaid.

Henrietta was not, then, at all hampered by the executor in the disposal of Congreve's property. Her own will was to show how faithfully she would carry out Congreve's wishes. After Congreve's death Henrietta asked her husband, as executor, to draw out and hold for her the three thousand pounds in Old South Sea Annuities which

Congreve had on deposit at the Bank of England.[21] Other funds amounting to £7300 she used to purchase a diamond necklace and ear rings.[22] "The Duchess showed me," said Dr. Young, "a diamond necklace . . . that cost seven thousand pounds, and was purchased with the money Congreve left her."[23] This purchase was sufficient evidence to Dr. Young that Congreve had been very foolish in leaving his money to Henrietta, feeling, no doubt, that she had merely squandered it on a bauble to feed her vanity for an hour. What Dr. Young had no means of knowing was that these diamonds were bought as a choice remembrance to pass along to Mary and to Mary's children. Henrietta's will specifically orders her executors "to assign my fine Brilliant Diamond Necklace which cost five thousand three hundred pounds and also the fine Diamond Ear Rings with Diamond Drops to them which cost two thousand pounds . . . to proper persons to be named by my Executors in Trust for the sole separate personal and peculiar use of my said daughter Mary." Then the Duchess went on in her will to stipulate that the diamonds should be passed on by Mary to some child of her own. Although Mary was only a child of eight when the will was drawn, the mother gave her power to change any one or more of the four executors who might happen to be negligent in carrying out the terms of the will.

Nor did the Duchess fail to pass along to her daughter Congreve's three thousand pounds in Old South Sea Annuities. The will stipulated that "the three thousand pounds which is mine and is now in the Hands of the said Francis Earl of Godolphin" must be paid "to my dearly beloved daughter Mary Godolphin." She also left in trust for Mary all her plate engraved "with Mr. Congreves Arms." And, finally, Henrietta specifically assigned to Mary "all Mr. Congreves Personal Estate that he left me."

V

In forgetting something of his youthful gallantry and devoting himself wholly to the Duchess, Congreve was not misplacing his trust. As his health became poorer, Henrietta became more attentive. When Congreve was at her lodge near Windsor Park in the late sum-

---

[21] For Congreve's three thousand pounds in Old South Sea Annuities see Bank of England, Folios 3/529 and 18/421. The funds were withdrawn for the Duchess of Marlborough on 12 February 1728/29.

[22] See the will of Henrietta, Duchess of Marlborough, dated 11 July 1732, proved 19 May 1736, at Somerset House, P. C. C., 113 Derby. A copy of the will is at the British Museum, Add. MSS. 28,071, ff. 34–39. It is significant, perhaps, that several years were allowed to pass after the death of Henrietta before the will was proved.

[23] See Spence, *Anecdotes*, ed. Singer, p. 376.

mer of 1726, he had a severe attack of the gout in the stomach, and his life was despaired of. Dr. Arbuthnot came out from London to attend him. Late in September Arbuthnot wrote to Swift: "I have been for near three weeks together every day at the Duchess of Marlborough's with Mr. Congreve, who has been likely to die with a fever, and the gout in his stomach; but he is better, and likely to do well."[24] He did improve, and by the end of November he was able to return to his lodgings in Surrey Street.[25] Swift showed much concern for his old friend and inquired repeatedly about his health. Next year, on getting a favorable report, Swift wrote to Pope: "Pray God continue and increase Mr. Congreve's amendment."[26]

But in 1728 Congreve's health was again so bad that he and the Duchess went away to Bath as early as April and remained very late.[27] The waters, however, proved to be of little benefit. "I am sorry," wrote Mrs. Howard to Gay, "the Bath is not of more use to Mr. Congreve; I beg you will make my compliments both to the Duchess of Marlborough and him."[28] Congreve and Henrietta were still there in October, when Lord Hervey complained that they were about the only people then at Bath "whose faces I know, whose names I ever heard, or who, I believe, have any names belonging to them; the rest are a swarm of wretched beings."[29] Well after the season was ended, the Duchess had stayed on with Congreve, hoping that the waters would do him good.

On his return to Surrey Street his health failed rapidly. The end was hastened, no doubt, by "the Accident of his being over-turn'd last Summer, in his Chariot at *Bath;* it was thought he had receiv'd some internal Bruise, because he often complain'd of a violent Pain in his Side."[30] He died early on Sunday morning, January 19, 1729. The following Saturday *The Daily Post-Boy* reported: "The Jerusalem Chamber of Westminster Abbey is now hanging with Black for the Funeral of Mr. Congreve, who is to be interred from thence next Sunday near the Cloister Door at the farther End of the South Isle."

---

[24] Swift's *Correspondence*, ed. Ball, III, 343; also III, 334, 340.

[25] On 22 November 1726 Congreve wrote from Surrey Street a letter to the Governor of the Bank of England. See above in Chapter XI, Note 15.

[26] *Correspondence*, III, 423.

[27] See Swift's *Correspondence*, IV, 16.

[28] *Letters To and From Henrietta, Countess of Suffolk, and Her Second Husband, The Hon. George Berkeley; From 1712 to 1767* (London, 1824), I, 298.

[29] See Lord Hervey's letter to Lady Mary Wortley Montagu in her *Works* (London, 1803), I, 87.

[30] See Charles Wilson, *Memoirs of the Life, Writings, and Amours of William Congreve*, Esq. (London, 1730), Part II, p. 151.

On the same day *The Flying Post* carried a summary of Congreve's life and gave details of his last illness: "He had for some Years laboured under a Complication of Distempers, attended with Lameness and Blindness, in which he was visited by several of the first Rank." The notice ended with the startling bit of news that "Her grace the Dutchess Dowager of Marlborough was with him . . . to the last." Startling to old Sarah at least! How she must have raged! Lady Irwin, better informed, wrote home: "The young Duchess [of Marlborough] has made herself very particular upon Mr. Congreve's death . . . The Duchess buried him very handsomely, and showed so great an affection for his dead body that she quitted her house and sat by his corpse till he was interred."[31]

The funeral was held on Sunday, a week after the poet's death. Congreve had said nothing about the place of his burial, only desiring that his body should be laid away in a plain and simple manner. But it was appropriate that he should be interred in Westminster Abbey and, as *The Daily Post* recorded, "with the usual Pomp and Solemnity." This is not to say that the Duchess put more of show than of sincere feeling into the ceremony. Her letter to one of the pall bearers, the Honorable George Berkeley, speaks for itself:

Jan. 22, 1728–9.

Sir,

I must desire you to be one of the six next Sunday upon this very melancholy occasion. I always used to think you had a respect for him, and I would not have any there that had not.

I am, &c.
Marlborough[32]

Another friend Henrietta asked to serve was, of course, Congreve's "Dear Dick" Temple, Viscount Cobbam. The body lay in state for three hours in the black-draped Jerusalem Chamber and then, between nine and ten in the evening, was interred "near [Sidney], the earl of Godolphin's Monument."[33] Two days after the funeral the Duchess wrote again to George Berkeley:

[31] Lady Irwin's letter is preserved at Castle Howard among the manuscripts of the Earl of Carlisle. See Hist. MSS. Com., *Fifteenth Report*, Appendix, Part VI (London, 1897), pp. 56, 57.

[32] Letters *To and From Henrietta, Countess of Suffolk*, I, 330, 331. The six pall bearers were the Duke of Bridgewater, the Earl of Godolphin, Viscount Cobham, Lord Wilmington, George Berkeley, Esq., and Brigadier-General Churchill.

[33] The exact place of interment and other details of the funeral were mentioned by *The Daily Journal*, 27 January 1729.

Jan. 28, 1728–9.

Sir,

The last letter I writ to you was upon always having thought that you had a respect, and a kind one, for Mr. Congreve. I dare say you believe I could sooner think of doing the most monstrous thing in the world than sending anything that was his, where I was not persuaded it would be valued. The number of them I think so of, are a mighty few indeed; therefore I must always be, in a particular manner,

Yours, &c.

Marlborough.[34]

Four years later Henrietta, Duchess of Marlborough, was buried very near to Congreve. For she had specified in her will—the same will in which she had passed along Congreve's estate to her daughter Mary—that her body should "be buried in Westminster Abbey in the very same place with the Right Honourable Sidney late Earl of Godolphin."

Whatever the feelings of the Honorable Francis Godolphin toward the lady who was his wife and the man who was devoted to her, he was too discreet to divulge them to an inquisitive and scandal-loving world. No doubt, mild gentleman that he was, a sense of decorum prompted him to direct in his will (as he did) that his body should be laid, not in Westminster Abbey, but in Kensington Church.[35]

It is simpler to read the mind and heart of Henrietta. The rare companionship that life had brought her was not to be frustrated even by death. She was no fumbler in her planning. Just as she had seen to it that Congreve was laid away in Westminster Abbey in accordance with what was seemly and befitting his greatness, even so she provided that her body was to be laid "in the very same place"—never to be carried away "at any time hereafter or on any pretense whatsoever." These earnest words were not to be ignored. In the near and quiet comradeship of the Abbey, the Duchess and Congreve have long been securely at rest.

[34] See the letters *To and From Henrietta, Countess of Suffolk*, I, 331.
[35] See the will of Francis, Earl of Godolphin, P. C. C., 16 Tyndal, Somerset House.

KEY TO THE MAP OF CONGREVE'S LONDON

(Congreve's Life at a Glance)

(From the Temple, at the Limits of the "City," westward
to St. James's Palace—a scant mile and a half)

*Bardsey, Yorkshire—nearly two hundred miles north of London. Congreve was born at Bardsey Grange on 24 January 1670 and baptized at the village church on 10 February 1670.

1. St. Paul's, Covent Garden. Congreve's sister Elizabeth was buried here on 22 September 1672.

*Ireland, Congreve's abode from his fourth to his nineteenth year, at Youghal, a seaport in the extreme southeast, 1674–1678.
Carrickfergus, a seaport in the extreme northeast, 1679–1681.
Kilkenny—at school, preparing for college, 1682–1685.
Dublin—at Trinity College, near Smock Alley, 1686–1688.

*Stretton Hall, Staffordshire—one hundred miles northwest of London —where Congreve probably tarried for a few months with his grandfather during 1689 and wrote *The Old Bachelor*.

2. The Middle Temple. Congreve was registered here on 17 March 1691— the second year after his arrival in London—and continued for three or four years a half-hearted study of the law.

3. Will's Coffeehouse, Covent Garden, where Congreve spent much time in the circle of Dryden to the neglect of the law.

4. Arundel Street, off the Strand, in which Congreve had lodgings with his old school friend and fellow Templar, Joseph Keally.

5. Howard Street. Here Anne Bracegirdle lived, just around the corner from Congreve's lodgings.

6. Charles Street, St. James's, site of the town house of Theophilus Hastings, seventh Earl of Huntingdon. This earl was the father of Congreve's cousin, the Lady Elizabeth Hastings, whom Congreve celebrated as Aspasia in *The Tatler*, Number 42.

7. Theatre Royal in Drury Lane, at which *The Old Bachelor* was first acted in March, 1693, and *The Double-Dealer* in November or December of the same year.

8. Lincoln's Inn Fields Theatre. Here Congreve produced his *Love for Love* (April 30, 1695), *The Mourning Bride* (February 27, 1697), *The Way of the World* (March, 1700), and enjoyed a full share with Betterton and Anne Bracegirdle in the profits of the company.

9. The Duke's Theatre in Dorset Garden, Fleet Street, where Congreve's masque, *The Judgment of Paris*, was performed in 1701.

* Starred entries—each placed in its proper chronological order—refer to significant places and events in Congreve's life outside of London. Numbers at the left of the entries refer to the map of Congreve's London.

10. The Queen's Theatre in the Haymarket—erected by the Kit-Cats in 1704–1705. Congreve and Vanbrugh were joint managers of this playhouse during 1705.

11. Jacob Tonson's shop "at the Judge's Head in Fleet Street," where Congreve's plays were printed and published. Before 1695 Tonson's shop was in Chancery Lane; after 1700, at Gray's Inn Gate.

12. Sheer (Shire) Lane, first meeting place of the Kit-Cat Club, where Congreve and other poets dined weekly at Tonson's expense on Christopher Cat's mutton pies.

13. The Fountain Tavern, in the Strand, whither Christopher Cat moved to entertain the Kit-Cats after many of the nobility had been admitted to the club.

14. Hackney Coach Office, at the foot of Surrey Street. Congreve was one of the five Commissioners (salary one hundred pounds yearly) from 1695 till 1705.

15. Wine Licensing Office, at the foot of Arundel Street. Congreve was a Commissioner (salary two hundred pounds yearly) from 1705 till 1714.

16. Button's Coffeehouse, opened in 1712 under the patronage of Addison, where Congreve sometimes joined Addison's "little Senate."

17. Tom Twining's Coffeehouse, in Devereux Court. Here Congreve purchased tea and "spaw" water.

18. Hoare's Bank, in Fleet Street, where Congreve—like Dryden, Betterton, Vanbrugh, and Wycherley—had an account.

19. Thomas Snow's Bank, in the Strand, through which Congreve probably conducted most of his affairs. (The Bank of England, in which Congreve had a large deposit at the time of his death, does not appear on the map since that bank was located in the heart of the City, about a mile east of the Temple.)

20. St. James's Palace, where Congreve—notwithstanding his declared aversion for court acquaintances—sought to further the political interests of Joseph Keally.

21. Godolphin House—to the left of St. James's Palace. Here Henrietta Godolphin (later Duchess of Marlborough) entertained Congreve in spite of the strong disapproval of her mother.

22. Marlborough House—to the right of St. James's Palace—built by the Duke in 1709, where the old Duchess Sarah lived on after her husband's death and raged at the reigning Duchess, whom she called "Congreve's Moll."

  *Bath—one hundred miles west of London—where Congreve spent his last summer (1728), as he had spent many before, in company with Henrietta, Duchess of Marlborough.

23. Surrey Street, off the Strand, in which Congreve had lodgings at the house of Edward Porter after 1706. Here Congreve sat with Swift

over many a bottle of cheap white wine, here he was visited by Voltaire, and here he died at five o'clock on Sunday morning, 19 January 1729, with the Duchess of Marlborough at his side.

24. Westminster Abbey, where Congreve was buried by the Duchess of Marlborough with great solemnity on 26 January 1729; and where, four years later, the Duchess was herself buried very near to Congreve.

THE FAMILY OF CONGREVE'S FATHER

Pedigree of the Congreve Family, of Congreve and Stretton, County Stafford, derived chiefly from the original manuscript record begun by Sampson Erdswick about 1593 and continued since, generation by generation,* with additions from William Berry's *County Genealogies* (1837), from *Alumni Oxonienses* (1887–1891), and *Alumni Cantabrigienses* (1922), and from parish registers and wills. In general only the main line of descent is shown, except for the period of the poet, when an effort is made to place all members of the family referred to in this biography.

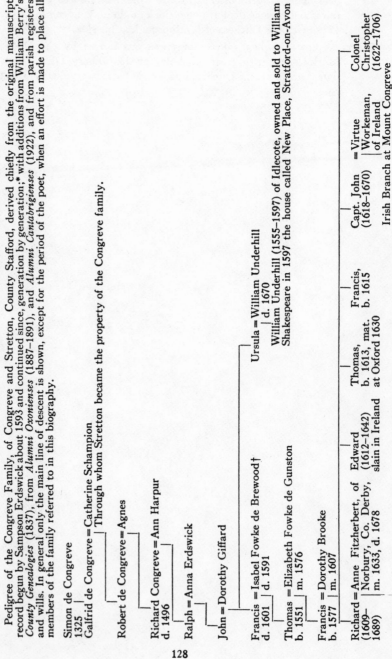

Simon de Congreve
1325
Galfrid de Congreve = Catherine Schampion
— Through whom Stretton became the property of the Congreve family.

Robert de Congreve = Agnes

Richard Congreve = Ann Harpur
d. 1496

Ralph = Anna Erdswick

John = Dorothy Giffard

Francis = Isabel Fowke de Brewood†
d. 1601

Thomas = Elizabeth Fowke de Gunston
b. 1551 | m. 1576

Francis = Dorothy Brooke
b. 1577 | m. 1607

Richard = Anne Fitzherbert, of
(1609–1689) Norbury, Co. Derby,
m. 1633, d. 1678

Ursula = William Underhill
d. 1670
William Underhill (1555–1597) of Idlecote, owned and sold to William
Shakespeare in 1597 the house called New Place, Stratford-on-Avon

Edward
(1612–1642)
slain in Ireland

Thomas,
b. 1613, mat.
at Oxford 1630

Francis,
b. 1615

Capt. John
(1618–1670)

= Virtue
Workeman,
of Ireland

Colonel
Christopher
(1622–1706)

Irish Branch at Mount Congreve

Colonel William = Mary Browning
(1637–1704?)   (c1636–1708?)

Elizabeth, buried at St. Paul's, Covent Garden, 22 Sept. 1672

William, the poet (1670–1729) d.s.p.

Carola = Clement Newth
b. 1648, m. 1687

Thomas b. 1640, B.A., Cambridge, 1662

Col. William, of Highgate, 1671–1746

William, b. about 1695, godson of the poet; officer in the army

Col. Ralph (1669–1715) = Anne Hanmer, m. 1717
Lt. Gov. of Gibraltar

Ralph (1722–1775) = Charlotte, sole heir of Sir Humphrey Foster, of Aldermaston House, Berks.
mat. Oxford, 1738; D.C.L., 1773; M.P. for Cardigan, 1764–74, d.s.p.

Anne d.s.p.

Richard (1714–1782) = Martha Jones, m. 1776
B.A., Oxford, 1736

Richard, b. 1778 = Mary Ann Birch, m. 1801, d. 1820

William Walter (1804–1864) = Anna Selina Bayly, m. 1830

William (1831–1902) = Fanny Emma Townsend, m. 1862

Gen. Walter Norris (1862–1927) = Celia Henrietta Dolores LaTouche, m. 1890

Sir Geoffrey, Bart., b. 1897

John b. 1636 dead by 1689 = Mary Nicholls, of Boycott, Co. Salop, d. 1706

John (1666–1729) = Abigail Harwood, d. 1752

Col. William (1699–1779) = Jane Waller d. 1790
sold Stretton 1733, d.s.p.

129

* For the use of this manuscript I am indebted to the kindness of Sir Geoffrey Congreve.
† This generation is omitted by Berry, but the diary of Thomas Congreve (born 1551) proves that Erdswick correctly includes it.

THE FAMILY OF CONGREVE'S MOTHER

Pedigree of the Lewis Family, of Yorkshire, derived from Joseph Hunter's *South Yorkshire* (1828) and the Visitations of Yorkshire in 1584/5, 1612, 1665/6, with some additions from parish registers, wills, and other sources.

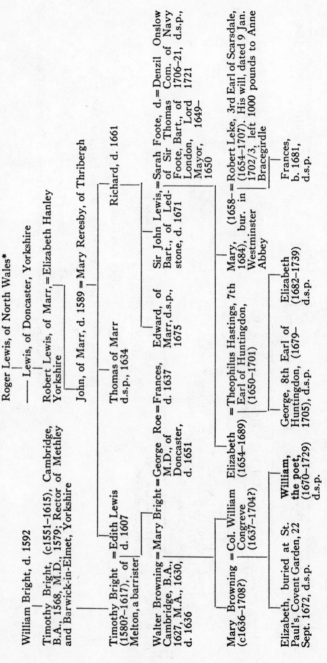

Roger Lewis, of North Wales*

—— Lewis, of Doncaster, Yorkshire

Robert Lewis, of Marr, = Elizabeth Hanley
Yorkshire

John, of Marr, d. 1589 = Mary Reresby, of Thribergh

Thomas of Marr   Richard, d. 1661
d.s.p., 1634

Edward, of   Sir John Lewis, = Sarah Foote, d. = Denzil Onslow
Marr, d.s.p.,   Bart., of Led-   of Sir Thomas   Com. of Navy
1675   stone, d. 1671   Foote, Bart., of 1706–21, d.s.p.,
                                      London, Lord   1721
                                      Mayor, 1649–
                                      1650

Mary, (1658– = Robert Leke, 3rd Earl of Scarsdale,
1684), bur. in   (1654–1707). His will, dated 9 Jan.
Westminster   1702/3, left 1000 pounds to Anne
Abbey   Bracegirdle

                  Frances,
                  b. 1681,
                  d.s.p.

William Bright, d. 1592

Timothy Bright, (c1551–1615), Cambridge,
B.A., 1568, M.D., 1579; Rector of Methley
and Barwick-in-Elmet, Yorkshire

Timothy Bright = Edith Lewis
(1580?–1617), of   d. 1607
Melton, a barrister

Walter Browning = Mary Bright = George Roe = Frances,
Cambridge, B.A.,   M.D., of   d. 1637
1627, M.A., 1630,   Doncaster,
d. 1636   d. 1651

Mary Browning = Col. William   Elizabeth   = Theophilus Hastings, 7th
(c1636–1708?)   Congreve   (1654–1689)   Earl of Huntingdon,
                (1637–1704?)   (1650–1701)

                                             George, 8th Earl of   Elizabeth
                                             Huntingdon, (1679–   (1682–1739)
                                             1705), d.s.p.   d.s.p.

Elizabeth, buried at St.   William,
Paul's, Covent Garden, 22 the poet,
Sept. 1672, d.s.p.   (1670–1729)
                           d.s.p.

* Seven preceding generations of this family in Wales are omitted here. For them see the Visitation of 1665/6.

130

GENERAL INDEX

Acres, W. Marston, 100n.

Addison, Joseph, 96, 97, 99, 108n.; comment on St. George Ashe, 25; praise of Congreve, 47; in Ireland, 83; loses his government offices, 85, 86 and n.; patron of Button's Coffeehouse, 126.

Aeneid, translated by Dryden, 39.

Agnes, wife of Robert de Congreve, 128.

Aldermaston House, 129.

Alexander, Sir Jerome, 23.

All Saints, Church of, at Bardsey, 6 and n.

Allen, Robert J., 75n.

America, Congreve documents in, xii, xvii.

American Council of Learned Societies, xvii.

Amsterdam, 94, 96.

Anne, Queen of England, 85, 86, 87, 89, 93, 96, 115; names Congreve and Vanbrugh, 67, 76.

Arbuthnot, Dr. John, despairs of Congreve's life, 121.

Archer, Simon, actor at Kilkenny, 21.

Argyle, Duke of, 107.

Aristotle, 64, 65.

Army, Irish, joined by Congreve's father, 7 and n.

Armytage, Sir George J., 30n.

Arran, Earl of, 17.

Arundel Street, London, 54; Congreve's residence in, 78, 79, 125; Congreve's removal from, 80; location of Wine Licensing Office, 126.

Ashbury, Charles, 27n.

Ashbury, Joseph, brings dramatic company to Kilkenny, 21; his company at Smock Alley Theatre, 26, 27n; and the Congreves, 28 and n.

Ashe, St. George, Congreve's tutor at Trinity College, Dublin, 24, 25 and n.; flees to England, 29.

Ashley, seat of Lord Shannon, 105, 115; Congreve writes letter from, 102; Congreve ill at, 102, 104.

Aspasia, title given to Lady Elizabeth Hastings, 125.

Athenian Society, The, Swift writes ode to, 48.

Aston, Anthony, 42n.; on Anne Bracegirdle, 43n., 44 and n.

Bagwell, Richard, 11n.

Baker, David E., on Congreve's quitting dramatic writing, 70 and n.

Baker Library, Harvard University, 99n.

Bale, John, gives plays in Kilkenny, 20.

Ball, F. Elrington, on Congreve's ballads, 90n.

Banim, John, describes Kilkenny College, 16 and n.

Bank of England, The, London, 34, 121n.; records at, xiv; confuses dramatist with his cousin, 33 and n.; Congreve's annuities at, 99, 120 and n.; Congreve's transactions with, 100 and n., 101, 126.

Bardsey, Yorkshire, xiii, 1, 5, 6 and n.

Bardsey Grange, birthplace of Congreve, 5, 6 and n., 7, 125.

Barn Elms, on the Thames, residence of Tonson, 96, 97, 98.

Barrett, Oliver W., manuscript collections, 88n.

Barrett, Roger W., 88n.

Barry, Elizabeth, 41n., 89; leading actress at Drury Lane, 43; member of new company, 51.

Barwick-in-Elmet, Yorkshire, residence of Dr. Timothy Bright, 1, 130.

131

British Museum, London, 3n., 30n., 39n., *passim.*

Brooke, Dorothy, 128.

Brown, Tom, 45n.; opinion of Anne Bracegirdle, 49 and n.

Browne, Reverend John, 16n.

Browning, Anne, mistaken for Congreve's mother, xii.

Browning, Mary, mother of Congreve, xii, 4ff.; mentioned in her father's will, 2 and n.; her education, 3; Tonson offers to entertain her, 55; at Lismore Castle, 55, 56; visited in Ireland by her son, 57; her genealogy, 129, 130.

Browning, W. E., 53n.

Browning, Walter, grandfather of Congreve, 2 and n., 3 and n., 4, 130.

Buck, Peter, 37n.

Burden, Godfrey, Congreve's schoolfellow, 22.

Burghley, Lord, 78.

Burkhead, Henry, 20n.

Burlington, Richard Boyle, second Earl of Cork and first of, 10; Congreve's father in the service of, 33, 55.

Burtchaell, G. D., 19n.

Burton, John, 6n.

Burton, Robert, 1.

Bushy Park, England, 104.

Buttery Book, Trinity College, Dublin, 23n., 24, 25, 26.

Button's Coffeehouse, frequented by Congreve, 126.

"Buxom Joan of Deptford," 90.

Byrch, John, 32.

Caius College, Cambridge, 62.

California, Congreve documents in, xii.

Calles, H. C., 71n.

Cambridge, England, 111.

Cambridge Festival of British music, 72.

Cambridge University, graduates of, Thomas Congreve, 129; Timothy Bright, 130; Walter Browning, 130.

Cardigan, 129.

Carlisle, Bishop of, 78.

Carrickfergus, Ireland, Congreve in residence at, xiii, 11 and n., 12, 14n., 125.

Castle Hill, Yorkshire, 6.

Cat, Christopher, and the Kit-Cat Club, 96, 126.

Chancery Lane, Tonson's shop in, 126.

Charles I, King of England, served by Captain John Congreve, 7.

Charles II, King of England, 14, 27, 91; loyalty of the Congreves to, 3, 4; his neglect of the loyal squires, 4n.; John Lewis knighted by, 5; return to England, 6; served by Captain John Congreve, 7; favors Viscount Ranelagh, 11; tennis enjoyed by, 13; interest in the theatre, 43, 51.

Charles Street, London, residence of the Earl of Huntingdon, 125.

Chartley Hall, Staffordshire, seat of Sir Geoffrey Congreve, xiv, 3n., 4n., 33n.

Chesterfield, Earl of, 111.

Chetwynd, Dorothea, 43.

Churchill, Brigadier-General, a pall-bearer at Congreve's funeral, 122n.

Cibber, Colley, 40, 41n., 42n, 45, 75; opinion of Doggett, 43; opinion of Anne Bracegirdle, 44, 49, 50 and n., 88 and n.; as Lord Touchwood, 48; on Congreve's share with Betterton, 52; on the success of *Love for Love*, 52; on the Collier controversy, 64; in *Squire Trelooby*, 73; on the Haymarket, 77; comment on Garrick, 89.

Cibber, Theophilus, on Congreve's quitting dramatic writing, 70 and n.; on Henrietta, Duchess of Marlborough, 110n.

"City," The, 125; location of the Bank of England, 126.

Civil War, The, the dramatist's mother during, 3; effect on the Congreve family, 3, 4, 5.

Clarea, W. D., paints portrait of Congreve, 6n., 45n.

INDEX TO MANUSCRIPT SOURCES

B. M., British Museum, London
P. C. C., Prerogative Court of Canterbury
P. R. O., Public Record Office, London
T. C. D., Trinity College, Dublin